# Problem Prospecting?!

*Completely Eradicate Your Prospecting Troubles By Leading With Problems*

*by*

Mark Ackers
Richard Smith
Stuart Taylor

*For every salesperson…*

*who has stared at the phone, too scared to pick it up*

*who has had their emails ignored*

*who has been ghosted by their prospects*

*who has been told to f\*\*k off on a cold call*

*This one's for you.*

This page was left blank intentionally.

This page was left blank intentionally.

# Foreword

Prospecting is tough. But, ironically, this is where we all start our sales careers. Regardless of the channel we choose, we are interrupting someone, trying (often desperately) to engage in a conversation meaningful enough to establish "a fit", "an opportunity" or a "problem" we can help solve.

And despite our years of prospecting experiences, this is a skill that is never truly mastered. It is an endless learning curve where the hard knocks and real-life experiences help refine the tactics and techniques that are most successful in a constantly changing world.

Congratulations. You have found a short-cut!

I first met Mark, Rich and Stu in interviews, over a decade ago, when they were looking to take the next steps in their burgeoning sales careers. I say next steps – Rich had a year's experience in customer service in an energy supplier's contact centre, Mark had done an internship in Marketing at a Premier League football club, while Stu had a few years selling cars and hospitality at the same club. If I tell you it was Sunderland AFC, you'll see that was a tough sell!

Why do I share this? Because over the last 15 years working with them, they have learned their considerable sales prospecting wisdom at the coalface, earning their stripes as reps, coaches and leaders, learning their craft with an insatiable appetite to improve and to help.

We started together in my previous start-up. Frankly, we were all learning on the job and we did more wrong than right, but we grew a business (The Test Factory – an online assessment platform) that worked globally with the likes of Microsoft, United Nations and the world's significant education publishers, bootstrapped but full of ambition, commitment and curiosity until we were acquired.

Our passion for sales naturally took us into solving problems for sales teams in our next venture, Refract – to improve sales conversations and outcomes. We'd seen the inefficiencies of sales coaching and researched enough to know that, for many, the problems were worse – what top performers did and what leads to successful outcomes has been a black box for most organisations.

And so, the path at the coalface got accelerated. Now we were seeing and analysing literally millions of prospecting conversations, working with hundreds of amazing sales leaders and many of the finest sales trainers and performance experts. We were no longer just learning from our own experiences and colleagues, but from a cast of thousands (tens of thousands, even), covering every type and stage of sales conversation, across industries and geographies, seeing the good, the bad and the ugly.

Today, as much as ever, they all practice what they preach: prospecting, coaching and learning. We coach each other, we share our best and worst moments, learning from our own mistakes and from the champagne moments of others.

This is why you need to read this book. They have condensed actionable insight into these pages, that will provide more impact on your sales prospecting than any other use of your time. These tips, takeaways and playbooks work.

It's not based on theory or methodologies, it's based on coalface prospecting. Their own, the colleagues they coach and the customers we analyze, to craft the tips and tactics that will improve you and your team's outreach and prospecting success.


**Kevin Beales**
**CEO**
**Refract**

# Table of Contents

# Introduction

A lot of people started out in sales by accident. Perhaps you did too?

We're yet to meet anyone who grew up wanting to work in sales. Most of us end up here by accident and leave within a few years. Many still believe in the old stereotype that the best salespeople are naturals who are born to do the job.

The truth is very different. Those that stick around are the ones who come to realise that sales is a skill, one that can be developed, and fine-tuned. They learn to treat the profession with respect, and recognise that a successful career in sales will open doors and deliver financial rewards that many careers do not. If being successful in sales was easy, everyone would do it. The good news is that everything in sales can be learnt. You just need to invest in your development.

The start of our career in sales was much the same as most salespeople. We were hired as "Business Development Executives" (or "Sales Development Representatives" in modern day terms). This means we were essentially responsible for creating qualified sales opportunities from a cold standing start. In other words we had to book meetings for more experienced colleagues to attend. Our induction in our new roles involved a couple of hours of product training; education on features and benefits; some detail on the market, and a lesson on competitors.

Once a few of these "on-boarding sessions" were complete, we were handed a laptop, a mobile phone, and shown to our desks. We were positioned in front of the sales whiteboard where we could see our names at the top, and a big old blank space underneath it.

"Crack on" was the message. Gulp.

All three of us have ridden the same train. We all fell into sales and, despite sharing similar experiences and frustrations throughout our careers, we've each managed to make somewhat of a success out of it. Prospecting (or top of funnel sales activity) is often seen as the toughest aspect of sales. It's often also looked on as being the least desirable part of the profession. Yet our collective appreciation that "nothing happens in sales until you generate an opportunity" has been key to our success. We vehemently believe that a fat pipeline can be the cure for most problems in sales.

Our journey can be broken down into two parts.

To start with we were left to figure it out for ourselves, as so many sales reps are: "There's a phone and a list of people to call – make it happen". Coupled with this, we were naïve, and if we're honest, a bit arrogant. We thought we knew it all. We believed that, to be a good salesperson all you needed was the "gift of the gab" and a polished slide deck with fancy client logos on it. Nobody told us any different and we did "okay", or at least enough to get by.

All three of us had managers. But our managers essentially sat us down once a week and read back to us what we could already see in the CRM, on the sales board, and on our commission sheets.

We were never taught how to make a cold call. We didn't know what to say when we were hit with specific objections. Our "elevator pitch" was essentially a fancy jargon-filled description of our product. Formal sales training was scarce and, when we received it, it was a one-off event with little lasting benefit. For us, it was largely a case of "winging it", and making far more mistakes than we were even aware of, losing countless opportunities in the process.

What we were lacking was a coach. Someone who would help us, and show us what we could do differently to get better results. We were left alone and had to figure out what we didn't know for ourselves. Unfortunately, this is all too common in our profession.

The second leg of the journey has been very different and for a number of reasons.

Above anything else, the world of prospecting and pipeline generation has evolved almost beyond recognition – particularly with the development of social media and digital selling. It has required an enormous amount of adaptation to remain current and up to date with the most effective techniques.

Secondly, all three of us have matured. We've taken our careers more seriously, and invested into our own development through books, podcasts, webinars and so forth. We are true students of the profession, always pushing ourselves to learn and develop. Just because we are "experienced", it doesn't mean we can't get better. But most importantly, we each have coaches. Someone who invests their time into our development every week. Not only that, but we have developed into coaches ourselves. We help our own team to avoid the mistakes we once made, and to continuously develop their skills and behaviours.

Each week we are immersing ourselves in reviewing each other's calls, emails, and outreach. We seek feedback from various sources on how we can tweak, refine, or overhaul our approach. We role-play with our colleagues. Yes that's right – we practice getting better. Look at any top athlete, singer, actor, surgeon, or lawyer. They all have one thing in common. They try to improve through practice almost every day, while working with a dedicated coach who constantly pushes and challenges them to do more.

If you want to get better at something, you need to be constantly self-reflecting and practicing.

Finally, despite the fact we have each now developed into sales leaders, there is one key reason why we're qualified to teach salespeople on how to be effective prospectors.

We still do it ourselves. Every single day.

**So why have we written this book?**

During the 2020 coronavirus pandemic and the subsequent economic downturn, we knew prospecting had become harder than ever before. So many sales professionals had been furloughed, but many were still working and being counted on to "sell their way" out of the situation. Companies were depending on their salespeople like never before. We knew that, in the hardest period of many sales reps' careers, they needed coaching, guidance, and support more than ever. Overnight, reps had been instructed to work from home, and they were now sitting in their spare bedrooms, trying to book meetings and close deals while being cut off from their colleagues and managers. The sales floor was gone.

We wanted to help. We knew we had the knowledge and experience to share with the sales community. So we decided to run a webinar – "Refract's Prospecting Bootcamp". This was a free online event through which we promised to share tips, tricks, plays and practical advice that anyone could take away and implement the very same day. Our USP was the fact we'd be sharing real clips from our own cold calls and presenting emails we'd sent to our own prospects. We wanted to prove we practice what we preach.

We had no Marketing spend or campaigns to drive attendees. All we had was our LinkedIn networks. All three of us posted a status and collectively agreed that if fifty people were to sign up, we'd be delighted.

Imagine our surprise when nearly a thousand sales professionals logged on to our Bootcamp!

After the event we were on a high. The amount of positive feedback we received was overwhelming. Many messages told us that our content was a huge helping hand during a worrying and anxious period. Seeing others take what they had learnt through our webinar and then putting it into practice (and reaping the rewards), fuelled us to run a second Bootcamp which had similar levels of attendees. We ended up running eleven Bootcamps in total and had thousands more sales professionals join us week after week.

We realised how many salespeople felt like we had all those years ago: desperate for coaching, and keen to learn and to discover new approaches they could use.

As a result of the staggering response to our online Bootcamps, we started asking each other what more we could do. We thought a book would be the perfect way to stitch together our collective knowledge, and here it is.

*Problem Prospecting?!* is both a question and a statement. We settled on the name for two reasons. Firstly, if you read and implement our advice then you'll eradicate any troubles you've ever had in making prospecting a successful, predictable, and repeatable process. Secondly, you will come to learn, chapter-by-chapter, that to capture the attention of your buyers, it is crucial to have a "problem first" mentality. In other words, focus less on your company and product, and more on the real problems your prospects are facing.

Whether you're just getting started in sales or twenty years into your career, this is a true how-to guide for the modern-day prospector. As with our online webinars, we've filled it with as much practical content as possible, along with every tip, trick and play we know of.

This book is the result of 30+ years of sales experience, lessons and learnings. It's also a labour of love, and one of our proudest achievements. We hope it serves you well in your prospecting efforts.

Go get 'em

Mark, Rich, Stu

N.B The makeup of this book has been a collaborative effort, with each chapter written individually which was then cross referenced and approved as a collective.

# Chapter One

# Know Your ICP

Your **Ideal Customer Profile** (ICP) is a description of the type of company that will gain most benefit from your product/service. These companies tend to have the most successful sales cycles, the greatest customer retention rates and the highest number of champions for your brand.

Before you can begin to even think about starting conversations with your target market, you have to know exactly who you're reaching out to. Once you've clearly identified your Ideal Customer Profile and understood what they care about, what they're trying to achieve, and the problems or challenges holding them back, then everything connected with prospecting gets easier.

As a sales professional, *don't think it isn't your job to identify your ICP,* and don't sit and wait to hear who Marketing thinks it is. Knowing who to sell to and where to focus your energy, effort, and time is *your* job. Don't rely on other departments and teams who don't have big revenue targets or KPIs over their heads.

If you don't know exactly who your ICP is, you run the risk of trying to be "all things to all people". I have been guilty of this in the past. I've worked for a number of companies that could theoretically provide their services to a lot of different "profiles", but here's the thing: different profiles come with:

- Different voices.
- Different needs.
- Different demands.
- Different problems.
- Different use cases.

These complexities can make your sale harder than it needs to be. You'll have a wider range of objections, different stakeholders, longer cycles, different competitors with different perceptions of the market, and so on.

Let's imagine you do win different profiles and secure them as customers. These voices, needs, demands, and use cases bring challenges for your Customer Success and Support teams. They could also derail your product roadmap as they have unique requirements: and if these aren't fulfilled it might lead to a painful breakup. As a result, this could mean they've actually cost your company money when everything is factored in.

Think of it the other way, if you have a super tight ICP, then everything is the same. Your prospects have the same problems that need solving. When your ICP has the same voice, needs, demands, and use case, you benefit in the following way:

- Your sales conversations are similar. You can master them and know where potential problems are.
- Your product team is focussed on building a product to serve one audience.
- Your Marketing speaks to the one type of customer. The language used is more compelling and relevant.
- Your Customer Success Team will also have better conversations, happier clients, and advocates, who get the most out of your product and will in turn rave about it to their colleagues and network.

Having a nailed down ICP is best summed up with the "Bus Driver Beach" analogy.

- You (Sales) are the bus driver
- Your Marketing department is advertising only one destination, i.e. the beach, as the ideal getaway for those who want some sun, sand, and sea.
- Customer Success are kitted out for a day at the beach – sun loungers, deckchairs, towels, sun cream, beachballs, buckets and spades… you name it, they have it covered.
- Your Product team is designing the perfect day at the beach for your customers.

Here's your ICP

- 18-30 years old.
- Overworked and underpaid.
- In desperate need of a day of relaxation.
- Keen on sunbathing, sand and ice creams.
- No driver's licence but lives near a bus stop.

How much easier is it for you to sell this ICP their bus ticket and a day out at the beach?

And here's the other thing. It's not only you who benefits. Your new customer is going to love the journey, the route takes them straight to the beach and, when they get there, it's exactly what you promised. Paradise.

And the situation is constantly getting better thanks to the joint vision you have with the product team. Customer Success is doing their bit too. They've kitted your customers out with everything they need, plus unexpected, bonus cocktails. Let's not forget about Marketing either. How easy is it for them to market to that specific ICP? And if they're half decent, they'll be generating inbound enquiries for you before long.

In this scenario your customers are also going to be so happy with their final experience, so selfies galore will be going up on Instagram and they will intentionally and inadvertently be telling other potential customers all about you and your service.

Nailing your ICP makes everything easier for everyone.

Now, let's stick with this analogy, but for a situation in which you're trying to be all things to all people.

You've got prospects who want to go to a museum, some who want to head to the cinema, and some who want to head to a shopping mall.

Your bus journey is going to suck. There will be too many stops so you can let people off. Some customers will want refunds; others will get to the beach and ask you to change the product. All the while, the Marketing team can't focus. It's a mess, and what's worse is that your Customer Service team ends up focusing too much on those unhappy clients. Your best customers, the ones who want to be at the beach, get neglected as a result. Perhaps another bus driver comes along and promises them a quieter beach, and one more to their taste.

I think I've made my point. One ICP and one destination makes it the best journey and destination ever. Nail your ICP.and only focus on those customers who want to go to the beach.

## How did we get our ICP?

About twelve months ago, we had a problem at Refract. We were trying to be all things to all people and to sell to anyone with a sales team. We were winning business, but we suffered from the problems we've just outlined.

So we decided to take action.

The sales team got together and tried to identify which of our clients were the "easiest" to win, which were staying with us, and which we were getting the most value from? We wrote a list, and then we started to discuss the things these clients had in common.

Within 90 minutes we had whittled it down to three ICPs, which was a significant improvement for us. But ideally you should have only one ICP, or a maximum of two.

Below are the three ICPs we created:

| Michelle | Dave | John |
|---|---|---|
| Sales Director. Inside Sales - Any Industry. Phone first. | VP of Sales. SAAS/Tech - UK & US (Not West Coast) | Owner. Sales Trainer UK & North America |
| · UK based | · 5+ Reps if VC Funded | · 2+ Employees OR |
| · 20-100 Sales Team | · 10+ Reps if bootstrapped | · Evidence of working with individual contributors |
| · Already record and/or listen to calls | · Coached SDR's &/or AE's | · Lists coaching as a service |
| · Annual Agreement | · In not annual, premium monthly commitment | · 6 month minimum contract |

We gave them names for a good reason. Going forward, we'd talk internally about ICPs as people: this can help those who aren't in sales get a feel for the types of clients we are targeting, and the names can be used across the business. It isn't essential to use names in this way, but I'd recommend them.

Here's a key sales lesson I learnt a while ago and one I wish I learnt on day one:

"Only spend your time selling to those who want to buy your product."

Nail your ICP and that's what you'll be doing. Time is a finite resource; don't waste it with the wrong people, instead sell to those who want a day at the beach. Look at your pipeline now, and be brutally honest with yourself about how many prospects simply aren't a great fit. These are hidden distractions which will hurt your results.

# Chapter Two

# How to Find Great Fit Prospects

Once you've identified your ICP, it's time to find as many relevant people for you to contact as possible. This can often be a challenge with so many prospects living and working in different places and companies. In this chapter we will help you use a variety of tactics and approaches so that you can find the very best prospects and start to generate conversations in next to no time.

## How to find leads

Leads are the lifeblood of any prospecting machine. Like anything, if you put garbage in, you get garbage out. You need a consistent flow of leads to feed the machine, but they need to be quality leads that match your ICP. There's no point wasting your time prospecting and chasing prospects that are never going to buy your product!

## Where do they hang out?

The first thing you need to know is not only who is my ideal customer, but also where are they? Are they vocal on LinkedIn? Are they members of a certain group? Do they spend a lot of time at events or trade shows? If you don't know, then find out. One good way is to speak with some of your current customers, if you're lucky enough to have some.

LinkedIn is the go-to for most people these days, and most of you reading this will find a steady flow of prospects from LinkedIn. With this platform, you can build a targeted prospecting list then use one of the various tools available to enrich this list with emails and contact numbers.

If you are planning on cold calling, which you'd better be, I'd strongly encourage you to invest in a tool that offers mobile numbers for your prospects. Without direct dials and mobiles, you'll waste far too long trying to find numbers and speaking with gatekeepers who are reluctant to transfer your call to the decision makers. The best way to get past the gatekeeper is to bypass them totally.

## Data Platforms

To be an efficient prospector, you need to automate anything you can so you can spend as much time as possible speaking with your prospects rather than completing tedious tasks. The good news is, there's more tech available than you can count today to help achieve this. I'll use this opportunity to talk through the tools the Refract team use because I've tested most, and can personally vouch for them.

Finding email and phone numbers - ZoomInfo, DiscoverOrg, LeadIQ. Hunter.io (email only).

I've a great deal of experience using all of the above, and without a doubt I've found LeadIQ to be the most effective and reliable, especially for mobile numbers. The data we use focuses mainly on the UK and the US, so I can't comment on the quality of data further afield.

If you're a manager asking your team to cold call, get them mobile numbers. If you're a rep being asked to cold call without it, then go and get a free trial of one of these tools so you can prove to your boss how much more productive and successful you'll be with decent data.

For more information on data platforms head to Chapter Sixteen..

**Virtual assistants**

If at all possible, use the services of a VA to help find data. It can be highly cost-effective, and if you do a little research you can find someone with a lot of experience building prospect lists. Upwork is our go to and we've got a couple of great VA's who we work with on a regular basis. Make sure you provide a strict brief for what you need and set them off on finding your prospect lists. Keep the lines of communication open between you to make sure you're getting the correct data. This may take a little longer at the outset however, once up and running, a VA through Upwork can be a prospector's secret weapon, saving you valuable time, and allowing you to focus on speaking with as many prospects as possible.

The third and final data source we rely on at Refract is Google. I'm sure most of you are aware of Google Alerts, which are a great way of getting notifications sent to your inbox every day. For those of you who aren't –

- Go to google.com/alerts in your browser.
- Enter a search term for the topic you want to track e.g. "Sales Coaching".
- Choose "Show Options" to narrow the alert to a specific source, language, and/or region.
- Select Create Alert.

That's it. This is a great way of getting up to date info on your prospects and trigger events that you can use to create killer personalization that gets their attention.

What most people aren't aware of is how you can use Google to search other sites such as LinkedIn or Twitter for example. This is a really powerful method where you can search for pretty much anything found on their social profiles. Using Google I can search LinkedIn to find a list of HR Directors in the UK, who love red wine and tiddlywinks. OK, it might be a small list but that personalised email has nearly written itself! This is covered in more detail later on in this chapter.

## Competitors of current customers

I've saved the best till last: my own favourite way to find your next best customer...

Get a list of every customer who works with you today. Then get your VA from Upwork to build a list of their top competitors.

Add to this list every time you bring a new customer on board, and start to record the reasons why they started working with you (refer to Chapter Fourteen for more detail here).

This makes your email so much more compelling. For example, do you think this would get the attention of the E-Commerce Director at Adidas:

'We're working with E-Commerce Directors at companies like Nike, helping them to increase sales online. Since working with us they've seen a 23.6% increase in online revenue. Would you be open to me sharing a couple of ideas how we're doing it?'
Do this first and your pipeline will be fuller than a centipede's sock drawer!

**LinkedIn (you will need a Sales Navigator licence for this section)**

While LinkedIn is already hugely powerful when it comes to finding good fit prospects, with some minor tweaks the impact can be significantly amplified and accelerated. The key to this are Boolean Searches (AKA Boolean Strings) within the keyword search box.

The keyword search box is largely ignored or at best used incorrectly. If salespeople use it, they will often type in a single word or phrase like. "coaching"

What this means is you're telling LinkedIn to only show you profiles that have the word "coaching" written on the individual's profile. While that will help narrow down your results, you can take this to the next level with Boolean Searches which are essentially a more complex search method which will return a better fit prospect for you.

Let me bring this to life with an example. At Refract, one of our ICPs is 'Michelle', a Sales Director who has a responsibility for coaching her inside sales teams. Those teams will make cold calls and/or run discovery calls and demos with prospects.

I could therefore type "coaching" into the keyword search box. However, with a Boolean search I can be a little more detailed and find the different variations of coaching. A Boolean search for me could therefore look like this:

("coaching" or "coach") AND ("inside sales" OR "discovery" OR "demo" OR "cold calling")

When entered into the keyword search bar, this essentially tells LinkedIn to show me all profiles where the word "coaching" or "coach" appears alongside other key words including "inside sales", "discovery", "demo" or "cold calling".

Now when you start to add additional filters like region, industry, company headcount, seniority level and job title, what you get back is often a perfect match.

Let me show you a search I'd use at Refract:

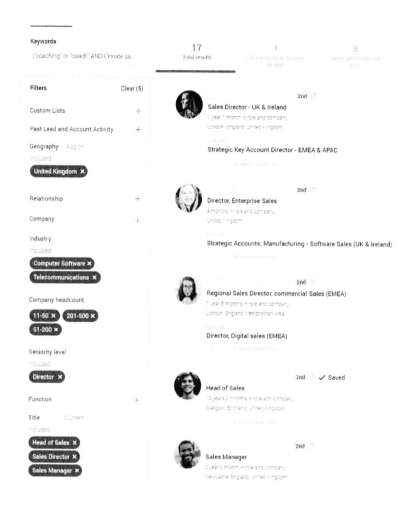

As you can see, my exact request to LinkedIn is to show me all LinkedIn profiles that are:

- Based in the UK.
- Within the Computer Software/ Telecommunications industry.
- A company headcount of 11-200.

- Director level.
- Job titles that include Sales.

That would already be a great, highly specific list, but I'm also only looking for the profiles which include the following words:

"coaching" or "coach", "inside sales", "discovery", "demo" or "cold calling".

As you can see it's returned seventeen results. All are perfect fit prospects AND I can personalise my approach at a high level, as I know they talk about coaching within their profile.

I would bend over backwards to speak to all the people on that list. And it's a list I created in less than 60 seconds.

**Top Tips:**

Do not put job titles as keywords. In my experience it simply doesn't work as well. Instead use keyword Boolean Searches that relate to interests and responsibilities.

You can also search for common interests, and it doesn't have to be work-related. Think red wine, golf, cheese, a football team etc. Imagine looking for your ideal job title, in your perfect region, with the right company headcount and on their profile they say they like "red wine" and "Manchester United". The list returned, is one of people you can write a highly personalised email to in seconds.

Here's another way to find ideal prospects on LinkedIn. And by ideal, I mean people who want your stuff!

Let's imagine you're a CRM provider and you want to find prospects who are looking for a new CRM system. Wouldn't it be awesome if you could find them? You can!

On the LinkedIn homepage, you'll notice a search bar – in this example you'd type in that bar "Recommend CRM" and then hit search. You'll now see some tabs appear underneath 'People', 'Jobs', 'Content' and 'More'. Hit the content tab.

If you followed those instructions, you'd see something like this

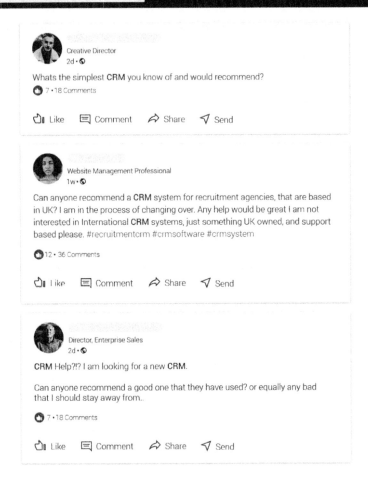

Creative Director
2d · 🌐

Whats the simplest **CRM** you know of and would recommend?

👍 7 · 18 Comments

👍 Like    💬 Comment    ↗ Share    ✈ Send

Website Management Professional
1w · 🌐

Can anyone recommend a **CRM** system for recruitment agencies, that are based in UK? I am in the process of changing over. Any help would be great I am not interested in International **CRM** systems, just something UK owned, and support based please. #recruitmentcrm #crmsoftware #crmsystem

👍 12 · 36 Comments

👍 I like    💬 Comment    ↗ Share    ✈ Send

Director, Enterprise Sales
2d · 🌐

**CRM** Help?!? I am looking for a new **CRM**.

Can anyone recommend a good one that they have used? or equally any bad that I should stay away from..

👍 7 · 18 Comments

👍 Like    💬 Comment    ↗ Share    ✈ Send

You can filter by "relevance" or "latest". I find relevance to be the best filter for accurate results.

You can see in this screenshot that we have three out of four people who have written a LinkedIn post

33

asking if anyone can recommend a CRM system. In my experience, when someone is posting for help, they have a problem they need to solve and you could be their knight in shining armour. The people writing these posts, as well as those engaging with the content, are perfect prospects for you to contact.

This method gives you ideal prospects as well as great timing. You know you're onto a winner when you reach out to a prospect and they reply with "this is a good time to speak". Normally, this doesn't happen very often because you can't control timing. With this method you can.

**Google**

Many do not realise that Google indexes LinkedIn like it does every other website. This means you can search LinkedIn pages in a highly advanced way.

To do this make sure you start at the Google website: www.google.com if you're in the US, www.google.co.uk if you're in the UK. The searches aren't as effective if you try to take shortcuts.

Then type the following into the Google Search Bar:

*Site:UK.Linkedin.com intitle: "enter a relevant word or phase here"*

*Note:* If you're not in the UK, swap the UK at the start for your domain i,e, ".CA" for Canada, "AU" for Australia or just LinkedIn.com for the US etc.

Let me bring this to life with a real example. At Refract we want to find people who have "Sales Excellence" in their title or on their profile. For us, that's a strong indicator that they're a good fit prospect as they're responsible for ensuring and improving "sales excellence". So I would type the following into Google Search:

*Site:UK.Linkedin.com intitle:"Sales Excellence"*

Google will then return all of the pages on UK LinkedIn that have "Sales Excellence" in the title of the page.

Google does what Google does best, it finds everything! In this example, it will find profiles with job titles that match, as well as articles, and so forth. What we need to do next is to refine our search. We need to tell Google what to filter out as, in the end, what we really want is perfect fit LinkedIn profiles.

The following phrase "-inurl" followed by what you're wanting to filter out, will do just that: it will filter out job listings, company pages, articles.

Therefore my search would be:

*Site:UK.Linkedin.com intitle:"Sales Excellence" -inurl:jobs -inurl:pulse -inurl:company*

Note: pulse = articles on LinkedIn.

And guess what, we're not done yet...

Remember our Boolean Searches? You can use them here too.

I might type something like this into Google...

*Site:UK.Linkedin.com intitle:"Sales Excellence" AND "golf" OR "Manchester United" OR "red wine" OR "cheese" -inurl:jobs -inurl:pulse -inurl:company*

Now imagine how specific and targeted my prospecting can get when I find a list of profiles, all containing sales excellence and a common interest, be that golf, Manchester United, red wine or cheese.

Not finding any results? Remove the specific interest and just use words like "enjoy" or "love" as shown below:

*Site:UK.Linkedin.com intitle:"sales excellence" -inurl:jobs -inurl:salary -inurl:pulse -inurl:company -inurl:showcase -inurl:blog -inurl:posts "enjoy" OR "love"*

This will return anyone with Sales Excellence in their profile and what they enjoy or love.

Want even more?

Remember our original search term:

*Site:UK.Linkedin.Com intitle:"enter a relevant word or phase here"*

LinkedIn.com could be replaced with Twitter.com. Yep, Google also indexes Twitter profiles meaning you can now search for prospects based on their bios and tweets!

Happy hunting. Go get em!!

# Chapter Three

# Nail Your Elevator Pitch

# (by Ditching the Pitch)

**What's the elevator pitch all about?**

Here's one definition I found:

*"An **elevator pitch** is a brief, persuasive **speech** that you use to spark interest in what your organization does"*

The problem with this definition is the word "persuasive". When we try to persuade people to do something, we're often met with resistance. Sales is not about persuasion. It's about helping. Furthermore, when we lead with persuasion, it often involves salespeople talking all about themselves or their product. So they are focusing on what they want rather than what their prospect needs.

This is the single biggest mistake salespeople make when delivering their elevator pitch. The pitch will be a confusing feature dump which just washes over prospects' heads, and triggers the dreaded objection that they aren't interested.

## Elevator pitch make-over

A recent coaching session involved a salesperson who wanted to sharpen up their elevator pitch. This is what it sounded like:

*"Dashboard-ly* is market leading technology which seamlessly integrates with your CRM and builds custom dashboards of all of the key metrics to help Sales and Marketing leaders with their reporting."*

Most elevator pitches fail because they sound like this. Here's my breakdown of what's wrong with the above:

*"Dashboard-ly is market leading technology"* – Your prospect really doesn't care if your product is "market leading". Moreover, it sounds over-hyped and focused on yourself. It's a recipe for turning your prospects off straight out of the gate

*"... seamlessly integrates with your CRM and builds custom dashboards of all of the key metrics"*

First and foremost, this is where the elevator pitch has turned into a product pitch. The salesperson is describing the *features* of their product as opposed to how they actually *help* people. Remember, people don't buy your features, they buy the outcome which your product will help deliver. Secondly, jargon like "seamlessly integrates" is unnecessary and potentially confusing.

Imagine that your elevator pitch is something you are going to deliver in a cold call when your window for grabbing attention will be small. Technical words are going to be wasted words as they will largely go over the prospect's head.

*"... to help Sales and Marketing leaders with their reporting"* - Here the salesperson believes they are explaining the problem their product solves. Where they go wrong here, is that *"helping with reporting"* is not a specific enough problem. In fact, it just describes a process. Your prospects aren't looking for help with reporting. They are looking for reduced stress, more time back in their day, and a better reputation within their company.

The aim of the elevator pitch is not to "throw up" your product all over your prospect's face. It's to succinctly and clearly explain how you help prospects tackle a specific problem, and get them "leaning in" to find out more.

Here's my makeover of the above elevator pitch:

*"We help time-precious Sales and Marketing Leaders, who previously got stressed from having to manually pick through their CRM each month for key data, to create important board reports. With Dashboard-ly, they get everything they need in one view, in seconds."*

Here's my breakdown of why this elevator pitch hits the right notes:

*"We help time-precious Sales and Marketing Leaders"* – I'm telling the prospect straight away that I help people just like them. I bring instant relevance to the table.

*"... who previously got stressed from having to manually pick through their CRM each month, for key data to create important board reports."* – I lead with the problems that my prospects face (in their own words) – manual jobs which take a lot of time, and –thus lead to stress.

*"With Dashboard-ly, they get everything they need in one view, in seconds."* – I haven't feature-bashed the prospect. I haven't told them all about integrations and dashboards. I haven't explained how my product works. I've simply told them the outcome of using my product and how it tackles their problem (all their data in one place in less time) in simplified language.

So remember:

- Make your pitch relevant. Start by saying who you help.
- Lead with the problems that your prospects face and use simplified language. A good rule of thumb here is thinking about how they would moan about that problem to their friends/ partner.
- Stop talking about your products features and benefits. Ditch the product pitch.
- Avoid jargon or technical words. Use simplified language – take your pitch back to primary school.
- Quickly and succinctly explain the result your prospects experience as an outcome of using your product. Avoid explaining 'how the product works'.

*Note: Dashboard-ly is fictitious.

## Practice Makes Perfect

Delivering a great elevator pitch is as much about HOW you say it, as opposed WHAT you say. Rushing through it, not pausing at key moments, and not putting emphasis on specific words can make even a well crafted elevator pitch sound tepid.

Like anything in life, practice makes perfect. It's absolutely crucial that you practice the delivery of your pitch, much like an actor will rehearse their script before filming. Buddy up with a colleague and practice together. Or, even better, record yourself and listen back. It's a great way of being more tuned in to what your prospect actually hears, and ensuring that you deliver your pitch fluently and with high impact.

# Chapter Four

# How to Cold Call like a Pro

## Purpose of the cold call

Contrary to popular belief, the purpose of making a cold call is not "to book a meeting".

The purpose of a cold call is to achieve the following

- To make them aware of you.
- To identify if they have problems they want to fix and make them aware of problems they do not realise they have or potential future problems.
- To make them aware you might have the answer to fixing these problems.
- To create interest.
- To create intrigue.
- To book the next step.

That's it.

If you can't identify problems they might have along with a desire to fix it, then qualify out.

Never, ever "force" in a meeting with someone by being pushy or by having "happy ears[1]".

When you force a meeting you are giving "fake news" to your boss. You also create false hope, and damage your credibility in the long term when they no-show and ghost you.

**A word of warning**

If you're in a lead generation role, it will be tempting to book in meetings for meetings sake. You get instant recognition and financial reward for booking it. I get it. I've done it. But it's short term gains, and the quality of your meetings along with "show-up" and conversion rates will suffer and be tracked.

Only book meetings with prospects you know your Business Development Manager/Account Executive/Closer can actually help.

---

[1] 'Happy ears is when a sales rep hears what they want to hear or makes assumptions based on what they heard.

If you're in a closing role and making cold calls for your own pipeline, remember your time is just as precious as your prospects. Only invest it with people you can help and who want help. Anything else is a waste of your biggest and most finite resource – time. You can't buy any more of it.

## Why cold calling isn't dead

I LOVE hearing that cold calling is dead.

The more people who think it's dead, the less my prospects are receiving cold calls and therein lies the opportunity for me to stand out.

For those who think it's dead I say this. Keep thinking it's dead, keep sending your emails, sitting waiting for a reply. The truth is, people who think it's dead only think that because they're rubbish at cold calling.

Cold calling, when done right, is the quickest way to build a good quality pipeline with legitimate opportunities. Fact. With the right mindset, data and dedication to attacking the phones you can book a number of meetings with people from your ICP who have problems they want to fix and think you can help. Unlike an email, cold calling provides you with instant feedback from your target market (good and bad), as well as a level of rapport that a faceless, voiceless message can't provide.

With cold calling, you can transform your pipeline in as little as one day.

## Power Hours

From experience, cold calling works best when it's done in time blocks. Cold calling done sporadically just isn't as effective.

**Why is this?**

Cold calling needs rhythm; it needs energy; you need to deliver your opening, value prop and closing like a pro. Think about it and consider any task. If you do it over and over in a block you get better at it. It's muscle memory. Cold calling is no different.

I also believe that, for most people, cold calling works best when there's a "mob mentality". One of the biggest reasons people don't like making calls is because the office is too quiet and they're worried people will be "listening in". I can sympathise with that type of self-consciousness but, ultimately it's an excuse.

What you need to do is block out a "power hour" in the calendar, twice a day. One in the morning and one in the afternoon. Come to those hours with a pre-built list of who you're going to call – I've found that twenty names is normally enough. In these power hours, you and your colleagues hit the phones together. Nothing else. No emails; no CRM updating; no distractions – just cold calling. The buzz of all doing it together can't be underestimated and you can really have a laugh, take the piss out of each other, and celebrate success. When done as a collective, it can be great fun.

If you can't do power hours with a colleague, still commit to doing them. Trust me: do it for 60 minutes twice a day, and in less than a week you'll see your pipeline transformed so it is filled with legitimate, qualified opportunities.

Like all prospecting avenues (including email and LinkedIn), cold calling is a numbers game. Do the maths. Two hours a day, ten hours a week, forty hours a month. It's more than enough to build a sustainable pipeline, particularly when you mix in your other prospecting channels. The key here is consistency and commitment. Failure to remain consistent will mean you only see peaks and troughs in your pipeline.

**Top Tips**

- **Prepare:** Turn up to every Power Hour with a list of people you want to call. They only last an hour, and while that is more than enough time for making cold calls, if you start adding research into that time block, you'll spend more time procrastinating than calling.

- **Protect the Power Hour:** See the Power Hour as a meeting, and a really important one at that. Decide that it can't and won't be moved. Do not book meetings over this hour. If you really have to, then make sure you find another time to do the Power Hour that day.

- **No excuses:** it's like going to the gym. If you miss a session, it is easier to miss a second and, before you know it, it's Sunday night, you've ordered a pizza and you're saying "start Monday". Don't miss your Power Hours. Give them the utmost respect.

- **Working remotely doesn't mean they can't happen:** At Refract, when we're all working from home we all jump on a Zoom call and run the sessions from home – remember 'mob mentality'.

If you don't dedicate the time to cold calling, it will inevitably never happen. Sporadic dialling just doesn't work – ultimately you're only letting yourself down.

## Mindset

There is a famous Henry Ford quote

*"Whether you think you can, or think you can't... you're right"*.

This nicely sums up how attitude and mindset determine success or failure.

Without an effective mindset, you will never be successful in sales. Hell, you'll never be successful in anything you do! Take cold calling, for example. I'm sure like me you've worked with talented sales reps who were crippled by the fear of picking up the phone. Michael Jordan once said *"you miss 100% of the shots you don't take"*. You can be the best cold caller in the world but if you don't make the dials then failure is guaranteed.

That's not to say failure is a bad thing. The easiest way to change your thought pattern is to celebrate failure. That might sound ridiculous but point me in the direction of the most successful people on the planet and I'll bet my mortgage they've failed more times than they can count.

A lot of sales reps also make the fatal mistake of putting their prospects on a pedestal. You need to forget their job title or the fancy suits your prospects may have: they are the same as me and you. Everyone of us has fears, anxieties and insecurities. Never think anyone is better than you, because they aren't!

You need to see yourself as being on a level with your prospects. You must get this into your head. Your time is as valuable as theirs, you know many things they don't, especially regarding your product or service, and it's your job to help them.

You need to pick up the phone with the confidence your product or service can change their world.

Think of yourself as a doctor calling a sick patient with a cure. This may sound extreme, but you need this level of confidence and belief in what you are offering. If you don't believe in your offer you're working for the wrong company.

As a sales professional it's your duty to help your prospects solve their challenges. Changing your mindset from selling to helping is a massive step in the right direction. When someone asks what you do, instead of telling them with what you do, tell them how you help.

Sales is helping people, simple as that.

Let's talk about fear. Fear is almost always irrational. Even when your fears are realised, the thought was still often far worse than the event itself. You need to keep this mindset when selling. I'll share with you three things that have helped massively in both my career and personal life.

1. The reason we suffer from anxiety is fear of the unknown. I always ask myself this question when I'm nervous about a big pitch or I am reluctant to pick up the phone – what's the worst that can happen?

The answer seems trivial and it is. The nasty Mrs Prospect might shout at me… Suck it up princess and pick up the phone!

2. Whenever I experience call reluctance, I think of the men and women who serve their countries dodging enemy bullets for a living so we can have our freedom. This brings me back to reality pretty quickly: my worries about making a call diminish immediately since I realise how pathetic I'm being.

3. Focus on what you can control. Too many people worry about things they have absolutely no control over. Will my prospect be an arse when he picks up the phone? Maybe, maybe not. None of us can predict the future, but what we can control is the act of picking up the phone in the first place. It's equally possible that the prospect is looking for a solution like yours and that your call will lead to him getting the promotion he's chasing. The most likely option is probably somewhere in the middle but you'll never know if you don't take that shot.

# How To Make A Cold Call

## Opening the call

When your prospect answers the phone and realises it's not their mother, husband or friend, their brain sets off an alarm and the barriers go up. These barriers are a defence mechanism: in order for you to get past them, prospects will immediately want to know:

- Who are you?
- Do I/should I know you?

So, when the line connects and you hear a "hello?" give them what they want and answer their questions before they ask you. The second they start asking you questions during the call opening like who you are and what you want you've lost control and are immediately on the back foot.

I start all of my cold calls in the exact same way and you should too. By disarming their "alarm"" straight out of the gate:

Prospect: *"Hello?"*

Me: *"Hi Mrs Prospect, my name is Mark Ackers and I'm calling from Refract, we've not spoken before..."*

Every part of that call opening has been carefully selected. I ensure that it's said in a really clear voice with a confident tone, and at a pace where they can actually hear and process what I'm saying.

Let me explain why this works

*"Hi Mrs Prospect"* – they know this call is for them and it's intentional.

*"My name is Mark Ackers and I'm calling from Refract"* – I've answered their first internal question, and by saying my name I've started the process of humanising myself. More on this in a second. By adding where I'm calling from and the company name, it achieves two things. Firstly they might recognise the brand in which case familiarity starts to kick in. Secondly, it's a slight nod that this is a sales call as I'm calling from a company and it subtly prepares them for that.

*"We've not spoken before"* – this part of the call is key. You are telling them that it's okay not to recognise your voice, and thus confirming this is your first

conversation. Doing this puts them at ease, as they're no longer scrambling around trying to quickly work out who you are and whether they should know you. So now with their initial questions answered, they're more relaxed and far more likely to be paying attention to what you say next.

## Pattern interrupt

It sounds obvious, but nobody is sitting there waiting for the phone to ring, especially from a salesperson.

You need to appreciate your prospect was probably right in the middle of something, no matter how trivial it was. To them, whatever they were focused on was more important than speaking with you. Although the call has now been opened, their barriers are still up and they are still somewhat distracted.

This puts you in a difficult position and this is where so many cold calls fail.

At this stage, not only is our prospect thinking of something else, with their barriers still up, there's also another wave of questions incoming. They now want to know:

- What do you want?
- How can I get you off the phone and get out of this unexpected situation?

**Keeping control of the call at this stage is key.**

We need to stick with the same approach by answering their questions before they ask them. Failure to do so will mean *they* take control of the call and you end up on the back foot. A key rule in sales is to always be in control of the sales process.

Here's what you need to do. Firstly, it's time to grab their full attention. All of it. We need them to forget what they were previously doing, and secondly we need to answer their next unspoken questions.

How do we grab their full attention?

**Pattern interrupts.**

A pattern interrupt is when you say something that grabs your prospect's full attention. You ask them a question or make a statement that they've not heard before. This requires them to shift their focus, and knocks them off their normal course of action.

Pattern interrupts are really common and you'll find them in almost every cold call. Typically however, they're weak and ineffective. Let me share with you some of the worst pattern interrupts you can use: you'll probably recognise them as you'll no doubt have been on the receiving end of them:

- Have I called at a good time?
- Have I called at a bad time?
- Have you got a minute?
- Have you got five minutes?
- How are you?
- Are you well?

These are all "canned" pattern interrupts. They stink of B2C telemarketing calls, and you will already be conditioned to respond to these questions with minimal thought.

Using a canned pattern interrupt means your prospect is not having to think, and therefore likely to still be focusing on whatever it was they were doing before. What's worse is that their cold-call alarms are immediately set off. A poor pattern interrupt typically leads to prospects taking control, and rattling off the classic objections in an attempt to get you off the phone. A good one disarms, takes prospects away from their objections, and invites you in to speak.

So what does a good pattern interrupt look like?

There's a few we use at Refract, and have split tested these over tons of calls to figure out the most successful:

- I just read your recent blog/Li post and I wanted to say thanks.
- This is a cold call, would you like to hang up?
- Are you in the mood for an ice-cold – cold call?
- From one sales professional to another can I tell you why I'm calling?
- I appreciate I'm an interruption to your morning.
- This is a sales call, but a carefully chosen one.

Our personal favourite is the one we coined two and a half years ago at Refract:

*"Have you got 35 seconds so I can tell you why I've chosen to call you."*

From time to time the team do use variations of time such as 27 seconds or 22 and a half seconds and have had great success with them but for me, 35 is the magic number.

Let me break down why this IS the magic number and the perfect pattern interrupt.

*"Have you got 35 seconds…"*

35 seconds sounds like a considered number. It doesn't sound like a gimmick like 22 and a half, and it also doesn't sound like a big ask like asking for a couple of minutes. It sounds like you're genuinely asking for just 35 seconds. In addition, it's an odd number. There's something about odd numbers, they stick in the mind a little more, feel more concrete and more effective in grabbing attention.

Over the last two years of cold calling, asking for 35 seconds has never, ever let me down. Sure, I've had people say "now's not a good time" (or similar), but I've always managed to have a conversation with them. Over this period I have never had someone say "no" with the call immediately ending.

*"…so I can tell you why I've chosen to call you."*

Humans are curious. Being curious, and not knowing the answer, is enough to drive you up the wall. This phrase piques their interest as they feel like they've been carefully selected. Everyone wants and NEEDS to know why they've been chosen and that's why, even if it's not a good time, they let me explain why I have chosen to call. In reality, they were just the next name on my hitlist!

What's really important with pattern interrupts is that you feel comfortable saying it. For example, some people will just not feel comfortable saying "this is a cold call, do you want to hang up?" and that's perfectly fine. Just pick the ones you're comfortable with, practice, and see what works for you.

**The Next Questions**

We have now begun, albeit loosely to answer their next questions of:

- What do you want?
- How can I get you off the phone and out of this unexpected situation?

The "35 seconds" pattern interrupt subtly implies that, once I've told you, the call is complete – even though it's just the start.

So to recap, here's how I open my cold calls:

*"Hi Mrs Prospect, my name is Mark Ackers and I'm calling from Refract, we've not spoken before. Can I take 35 seconds to explain why I've chosen to call you?"*

**Want to take it up a gear?**

Add in "from one XYZ professional to another". So for me it would sound like this:

*"Hi Mrs Prospect, my name is Mark Ackers and I'm calling from Refract, we've not spoken before.* **From one sales professional to another,** *can I take 35 seconds to explain why I've chosen to call you?"*

BOOM. You've just humanised yourself even further, and put yourself on their level. In their mind you're now both sales professionals You're just like them. You've walked in each other's shoes.

When they hear this, most people tell me "but I'm in sales and I sell to finance / Marketing / HR professionals etc, I can't say that". YES. YOU. CAN.

From one Finance expert to another

From one Marketing expert to another

From one HR professional to another

Do you sell to that profession? Then you are an expert.

With that additional touch it's all there.

- **Empathy** (we're both in the same boat).
- **Familiarity** (people like people they believe to be similar).
- **Humanisation** (we're both walking in the same shoes).

And that is how you open your cold calls.

- You keep control.
- You grasp their full attention.
- You lower their resistance and anxiety.
- You answer their questions, without them having to ask.

- You're on a solid footing: you've humanised yourself; you've built credibility and empathy.
- You get permission to actually tell them why you've chosen to call.

Now what?

**Value proposition – lead with problems**

So now they've given you permission to tell them why you're calling.

This is where most sales reps fail. Most will start to talk about their favourite subject – themselves and their company. It will sound something like this:

- "We work with {enter household names here}"
- "We're an award-winning..."
- "We achieve ABC results..."
- "We save you time and money by..."

Do you think at this specific point of the phone call they truly care about your company awards? Do they really believe you can save them time and money when you know nothing about them?

Rolling straight into a product pitch, listing features and nuggets of information is what often follows next. Yet most of the time the prospect is just hearing white noise. At best the odd word makes sense to them.

It's almost like the rep feels they need to build credibility for their company, despite the fact they've already achieved this with an impactful call opening.

The harsh reality is that your prospect doesn't care. Like you, their favourite subject is themselves. So focus on that.

Everyone you speak with has something they need to achieve in their role, and that's what they care about. When they hear your value proposition, you need to get them pondering:

- Can this make me better, more successful, or happier?
- Do I have a problem they can fix?
- Does this sound like someone who understands my world?

Of course there is also the possibility that they aren't even aware of a problem they have, and your value proposition is the "lightbulb moment".

Here's what you need to do.

It's *paramount* that you lead with problems, and see if those problems resonate with the prospect. Here's the bottom line. If your prospect doesn't have a problem that they are motivated to solve, you're not getting a sale. So stop wasting your time (and theirs) as soon as possible.

To bring this to life let's look at how an average sales rep pitches as opposed to how a great rep does. I'm giving full credit for this example to Sales Expert, Josh Braun.

Let's imagine both sales reps sell "Fire Flowers" and that each rep is going to cold call everyone's favourite Italian plumber – Super Mario.

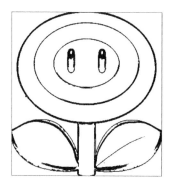

**Typical Rep:** *"We have these awesome Fire Flowers, voted number one in the world by Nintendo and they're used by Sonic and Pac-Man. When these guys eat our Fire Flowers they become big and strong. Right now we're doing a promotion of buy one get one free. Would you like to try some?"*

**Great Rep:** *"I was curious to understand if like many others in Mushroom Kingdom, you're constantly waking up to find Bowser has kidnapped Princess Peach and, frustratingly, it's costing you on average five lives to save her, defeat your enemy and complete the game. Is this something that you're bumping into?"*

The **Typical Rep** is talking about his favourite subject- themselves, their company, and product. It's a classic "features and benefits pitch" telling the prospect that the product will make him big and strong. But that isn't the problem Mario is facing. He wants to save Princess Peach and complete the level.

The **Great Rep** is helping Mario realise there's an easier, better way to achieve his ultimate goal. But he is doing more than that: he is telling Mario that he's an expert, he knows his world and the specific problems he faces, and the number of lives he normally requires. The rep isn't being pushy or assumptive as he's asking whether the problems he's aware of actually resonate with Mario? Maybe Mario only uses one life? Maybe he's not interested in Princess Peach and Yoshi is his main love (in the year 2020 you just never know!)? Ultimately, from Mario's response, the Great Rep will know if this is a problem he has and is motivated to fix it.

When you lead with problems, you continue to build credibility and rapport. The key to this is knowing what problem you can solve, and it's important you get this right. Let me give you some other real life examples:

- A dentist fits mouth braces but that's not what he sells. He sells perfect smiles – that's why people get braces.
- Locksmiths provide locks but that's not what people buy. They buy security and a feeling of safety.
- Babysitters sell their time and look after your child. But people are buying a night out with their partner.
- Hotels sell rooms. But people buy a romantic weekend away.

- Diet pills sell weight loss. But people buy them because they want to look good in their bikini or they want more matches on Tinder etc.

Identifying the problems and reasons why customers buy took us a little longer than we'd like to admit at Refract. As reps we could have said we provided a number of things:

- A sales call coaching platform
- Insight into call recordings
- Analysis of conversations at scale
- Trends of the sales team
- Quicker access to calls

The list was endless. But when we break it down, people actually buy Refract because they want to generate more revenue.

Once we nailed our ICPs along with the problems we actually solve for them, our conversations became so much easier, as did our product roadmap and Marketing message.

Let me share with you an example of how we'd lead with problems for one of our ICPs:

# Michelle

Sales Director. Inside Sales -
Any Industry. Phone first.

- · UK based
- · 20-100 Sales Team
- · Already record and/or
  listen to calls
- · Annual Agreement

In this example our ICP is Michelle, Sales Director for a Contact Centre.

**Me:** *"Hi Michelle, my name is Mark Ackers and I'm calling from Refract, we've not spoken before. From one Sales Professional to another, can I take 35 seconds to explain why I've chosen to call you?"*

**Michelle:** *"Sure."*

**Me**: *"I appreciate it, I speak with a lot of successful sales leaders who all have high performing telesales teams and yet, they're facing a couple of key challenges*

1.      *The uncomfortable truth is they know deep down every day their reps are making mistakes on their calls that result in revenue being lost. They're also missing opportunities to cross-sell and upsell and it's a frustration, as fixing this would help them achieve their Q2 targets.*

2.      *The other is that it takes new hires too long to hit revenue targets consistently.*

*I don't suppose either of those resonates with you at all, Michelle?"*

**Michelle:** *"Yeah, they do."*

**Me:** *"Interesting, can you tell me a little more about that?/could you give me a recent example?"*

**Michelle:** (will then explain the situation)

Notice how I never spoke about Refract. I didn't mention what our platform does or really get into any level of detail. I simply spoke to Michelle about her world, her problems, and that I might have a solution for her.

A key exercise you should do is to write down the top one or two problems you solve for your clients, and weave that into your value proposition.

## Closing off and suggesting next steps

Once you've shared your key problems and they've confirmed these are problems they're facing, it is time to start planning your exit strategy. This is not the moment to waffle on. Remember the goal of a cold call is simple – to find people who have a problem you might be able to solve. Nothing else needs to be achieved at this point.

Here's how my conversation with Michelle would typically continue:

**Me:** *"I know I've called you up out of the blue, but we're helping sales leaders like yourself completely eradicate these challenges. I'd like to suggest we set up a call where I can share a couple of ideas with you that might not be on your radar, and together we can explore a fit, does that sound fair?"*

**Michelle:** *"Yes"*

**Me:** *"Great, do you have your calendar available, next Wednesday at 4pm is open for me, you?"*

This 'closing the call' play works because it's conversational, it doesn't feel salesy, and I still haven't really talked about our product or services. All Michelle knows at this stage is that we might have the answer to her problems.

Let me break down the key components of my "close":

- **Sales leaders like you:** it's relevant to her and we sound like we're experts. We're doing this day in day out – does she want to miss out?
- **Completely eradicate:** I learnt this phrase from Chris Beall of ConnectAndSell. It tells your prospect this problem can completely disappear for good. It feels concrete.
- **I'd like to suggest:** it sounds consultative and not pushy.
- **A couple of ideas:** people like to hear ideas. They sound fresh and new.
- **Might not be on your radar:** it teases that they're likely to have not even thought of this before and thus builds curiosity.
- **Sound fair?** – Everyone wants to be fair, and you've just described why they should speak with you again.

You'll notice I then ask if their calendar is available and suggest a specific time and date. Although standard practice, what's key is I'm suggesting something as soon as possible, such as the next day. If I'm speaking with them in the morning, I'll even shoot for the afternoon.

The reason I suggest a date as early as possible is that this subtly bends their reality and anchors their mind to picking something in the immediate future. Right now, their interest is as high as it's ever going to be. So strike while the iron is hot.

I learnt from experience that when I asked the question: "when works for you?" the prospect would naturally look to next week or the week after. They subconsciously convince themselves that they are too busy right now, so they will naturally push it out a week or two, when their calendar usually has more free space than they let on.

Another key note. Letting them push it back a week or two also adds a week or two to your sales cycle. The old sales adage that "time kills deals" is as true today as it always has been. Also, the further out the next step is scheduled, the greater the likelihood of that call being moved or cancelled.

**Want to take it up a gear?**

When you get a little more comfortable, it's okay to ask your prospect a couple more questions on an initial cold call. The key is what and when.

Once you've shared the problems you help solve, and they have confirmed they exist in their world, you can ask a couple of questions, just don't overdo it. Don't turn this into a discovery call. I repeat, don't turn this into a discovery call. No matter how well the conversation is flowing – always remember the key objective of the cold call.

Use a few extra questions to qualify a little harder and confirm that these are real problems with real consequences. A prospect will only buy if they NEED to fix the problem, and it's on their priority list. Here's a few questions I'd use at this stage:

- Out of the two problems I've shared, is there one in particular you're running into the most?
- Can you give me a recent example?
- Have you tried fixing this before?
- If you could fix this, what would it mean for you?

There is one other window to ask a couple of questions in the initial cold call. That's after you've confirmed the next step. Once the next step is agreed, both you and the prospect are more relaxed, and so it becomes easier to gather some additional information.

Once we've agreed a time and a date for the next step, I'll say the following to prepare my prospect for the fact that some more questions are coming:

*'So I can make our next call super relevant for you, can I just check a couple of things?'*

They never say no to this. They're already committed to the next step, and who doesn't want to make the next conversation super relevant? At this stage ask two to four questions that will help you properly prepare, but DON'T ask "commission breath" questions like these:

- How big is your team?
- Do you have a budget?
- Who signs the order form?

Instead, I'd ask the following questions:

- Do you record your team's conversations at the moment?
- What do you do with those recordings?
- Does anyone else use them?
- Out of interest, the problems you're facing, who else cares about solving that?
- Where does solving this sit on your priority list?
- Before we next speak, is there anything else you think I need to know?

## Cold Calling Pitfalls

Throughout the next passage of this chapter I've listed the potential pitfalls of the cold call:

- Weak call opening/pattern interrupt.
- Pitching.
- Losing control.
- Turning the cold call into a discovery.
- Booking the next step too far into the future.
- Caring about the outcome.

**Weak call opening/ pattern interrupt**

Remember when the call connects – stay in control. Start working on their barriers by giving them the information they need, in a nice, clear way. Too often sales reps can start their call sounding timid, weak and unsure. The best way to get this right is simple. Practice. If you're looking for perfection you're going to be gutted. I've been cold calling for over ten years and I still make mistakes. Yet you could wake me up at 2am, and the vast majority of the time I could tell you what I'd say on a cold call in a split second because it's muscle memory. Like anything in life, if you want to get good you have to practice, practice some more, and then practice again. Never stop.

A lot of sales reps are too proud to practice. They find it "cringy" or it makes them feel uncomfortable. The reality is they just need to get over themselves. However, I'd imagine anyone who has made a decision to buy and read this book does not feel this way but will know many who do.

**Pitching**

Premature product pitching is one of the two biggest reasons cold calls fail. Nobody likes being pitched.

Everyone does, however, like hearing about their favourite subject – themselves. Lead with their problems, talk about their world and the fact that you can completely eradicate their pain points, making them happier and better in their role at the same time. That's what your prospect wants to hear. They don't want to hear about your product. Not yet, anyway.

**Losing control**

If you lose control in a cold call you're toast. You lose control when the prospect feels under pressure and/or when they sense you're not entirely convinced yourself. You lose control when the prospect starts asking you questions and you end up on the back foot. One of the key ways to avoid being asked questions is by telling them what they want to know. Who, Where? Why?

The only question you want to hear is "How do you do that?" or similar.

**Turning the cold call into a discovery**

This is a balancing act and only you can know when you're going into discovery mode. The purpose of the cold call is really simple: confirm a problem, create interest and book the next step. The discovery stage in the sales process is a crucial step and one which deserves its own dedicated time and focus, where both parties have committed to the conversation. Do not dilute this stage by turning your cold call into a discovery meeting.

**Booking the next step way into the future**

Time kills deals. It's that simple. The longer the gap between each conversation, the more the prospect will forget, the more their excitement dwindles, and the higher the risk of "ghosting" or the opportunity collapsing.

Book the next call <u>as soon as possible</u>. If they push back and want it 3/4 weeks into the future (or longer!) challenge them, and ask outright the reason behind the delay. Be flexible. (For instance, offer to do the call before or after work at 8/8.30am or 5pm). Another great time we've found is suggesting "just before lunch".

**Caring about the outcome**

This is the second key reason cold calls fail. Reps are too busy caring about the outcome and that means they're focussed on their own needs and wants (like KPI's, commission etc) rather than the prospects.

If the outcome is "no next step", it means it's not something they need (or you cocked up – it happens!). If they don't need your product, <u>find out now</u>, and not in three months' time.

When you detach yourself from the outcome, cold calling immediately gets easier.

The way I see it – the next "no", just gets me to the next "yes" faster. I only want to speak with people who want to speak with me.

Stop trying to sell your product to people who will never buy it. Imagine if you could spend all your time with people who are genuinely interested, and have real problems you can solve?!

## Recording your sales calls

The greatest athletes in the World all record themselves and watch "Game Tape" to help themselves get better.

Hall of Fame NFL Quarterback Peyton Manning was infamous for his obsession with devouring recordings of his performances, as he was determined to find ways he could get better.

Every single top flight football manager and team watches recordings of their matches and training sessions to reflect on what didn't work out, and how to adapt or overhaul it.

Every professional golfer records their swing, so they can measure and fine-tune to achieve those marginal gains.

So it always staggers me that recording of sales calls is seen as such an alien concept to so many in the sales profession.

If you want to get better at something, you HAVE to self-reflect. However, reflecting on your sales calls without the ability to listen back is very hard to do.

I remember when I first listened back to my sales calls. It was uncomfortable. I realised I was talking far more than I thought I was. I started hearing crucial things my prospect was saying that I had clearly missed the first time round. I recognised that my call openings were rushed and often difficult to understand.

The long and short of it was that I was damaging my success purely because what I thought I was doing in my sales conversations was very different to the reality.

Being able to record, listen back, and have others listen to my sales calls to give me feedback has been the single biggest reason for me getting better at sales over the past five years or so. Great tools like Refract are helpful here too of course.

## What do you do if you muck up a cold call?

It's really easy... call them back at a later date! Here's a story of when I bombed a cold call.

I don't really know why what happened, happened but I didn't follow my normal process. I can only imagine it's the same as when a footballer changes his mind in the run up to a penalty (I've fluffed a lot of them as well!).

I was put in my place and told by my prospect to "send an email" - I saw it as my 'punishment' for a poor cold call. It was no surprise I received no response to my email.

After four weeks, I called back and booked a meeting. Below is the opening transcript:

*"Good afternoon, it's Mark Ackers from Refract. I don't expect you to remember me but I called you about four weeks ago and did a pretty crappy job of it. Would it be ridiculous of me to ask for a shot at redemption?"*

My call opening was greeted with laughter. It was a short call. One minute and twenty three seconds to be precise. We booked a call in the calendar for the following week.

Always remember, when it comes to cold calling the biggest barrier to success is your own self-limiting belief.

You will make mistakes and fluff cold calls, but that doesn't mean the person you were calling is no longer a good fit. Give it a few weeks and call back, hold your hands up, and ask again. Self deprecation will humanise you and has a funny way of getting prospects treating you like a human being, and giving you a second shot.

Fortunes are made in the follow up. Never forget that.

Time for you to start calling back those hang ups...

# Chapter Five

# Dealing with Gatekeepers

The easiest way to deal with gatekeepers is to avoid them. I know, I know, easier said than done. However if you invest in a decent data provider with direct dials and, even better, mobile numbers, the amount of gatekeepers you'll come across should be significantly reduced.

However, we obviously still need to work out how to speak with gatekeepers as we won't be able to get mobile numbers for every prospect.

Here's the exact script I use when I sense a gatekeeper has picked up the phone.

*"Morning/Afternoon Hannah it's Stu from Refract, is Chris about please?"*

Let's break down why this works.

Firstly, when they answer the phone, make sure you listen out for their name. Most companies will answer with something like 'It's Hannah from ABC how can I help?'

Ensure you use their name in a familiar tone. Trust me, it'll help. Dale Carnegie told us all that the sound of a person's own name is the most precious thing to them. So take this opportunity right at the beginning of the call to make yourself sound familiar and human.

Next, I say who I am and where I'm calling from... I do this for a couple of reasons.

Firstly, the person on the other end of the line is starting to wonder if they know me or not, because I come across so familiar.

Secondly, most gatekeeper's first question will be to ask who's calling. If they don't ask that, typically they go to default question number two: "where are you calling from?" Boom, we've disarmed the first two questions out the gate before they have even had a chance to ask them. Do this right and we've got the gatekeeper on the back foot and taken them out of auto-response mode.

With this opener, I've disarmed their go-to questions. Often the response I get to this is "erm yeah, I'll just see if she's free."

This method works well in practice, but it's far from foolproof. The reality is, nothing is foolproof in sales. So we need to prepare some more options. The one thing every gatekeeper has left in their armory is the dreaded "Can I ask what the call's regarding?"

A little voice in your head is probably screaming "no you can't!" but as much as you'd love to scream that down the phone, it's not a wise response if you want the gatekeeper to help you out and transfer your call.

Instead, keep calm and politely reply with the reason for your call.

Here's your chance to sound like an expert and mention something only your prospect would be responsible for:

*"I need to speak with Steve regarding the contract terms of company cars? Is that something you can help me with instead, Hannah?"*

Why does this work?

Firstly, we've mentioned a genuine reason for the call, one that Steve will most likely be responsible for. If he isn't, then we shouldn't be ringing him in the first place. Secondly, we've appealed for help from the gatekeeper, but the natural response from them will be to tell us that they can't help, and that Steve is our man. More often than not they'll do as you ask and transfer the call. In short, the gatekeeper panics that you are going to ask difficult questions they won't have the answer to.

Some will, some won't, and the most seasoned gatekeepers will often hit you with the dreaded:

*"Can you send some information to info@abc.com please?"*

Never send emails to generic inboxes like this. It's an absolute waste of time. Try this instead.

*"Hannah, I appreciate you have a hard job to do and screen calls for Steve, however we're helping companies like A, B, & C and I really think Steve needs to hear about how we can potentially help. Is it fair to say that if I were to send an email to that address I'd have more chance of winning the lottery than getting a reply?"*

Let them answer and most will either agree, or say no – that email inbox is often checked.

Here's your chance to appeal for help:

*"If you were me Hannah, how would you go about getting in touch with Steve if you had an idea he really must hear?"*

This works because it puts the gatekeeper in your shoes and appeals to their human nature to help.

Another response gatekeepers will often use is:

*"Sorry, its company policy that we don't transfer calls/give out numbers"*

This is a tough one, but I have something you can try. It won't work all the time but it does have a small success rate:

*"Understood, have you ever made an exception?"*

Then shut up.

What's happening now, is the gatekeeper is starting to think about when they have made an exception and/or the reason they did. This means they'll be more likely to help you out.

I use this all the time and not only with gatekeepers. I use it when buying pretty much anything, to my wife's constant embarrassment, and it's saved me a fortune on cars, carpets, and even my house.

We won't get past every gatekeeper, but practicing and applying the tips above will significantly improve our chances. As with anything on the phone, it's all about the delivery, so working on your tone and confidence is paramount.

# Chapter Six

# Leaving Better Voicemails

The vast majority of sales reps do not leave voicemails and those that do tend to leave ineffective ones.

First of all, should we be leaving voicemails? Yes. Debate over.

Think about it, by the time you hear the beep, you've done the hard part.

- You've found a prospect.
- You've done some research (and some of you LOVE to spend an age on research).
- You've decided they're worth speaking with.
- You've dialled their number.

A good voicemail takes 20-30 seconds so, given the investment you've made to get to this point, why aren't you taking this free shot at getting their attention?

The answer to this is that most people don't know what to say or have ever had any success from leaving one, so they don't see the point. So most people don't leave one at all.

**Here's a few examples of infective voicemails**

*"Hi [Name], It's Mark Ackers Calling from Refract on 07805410197, that's 07805410197 I'm calling because I wanted to speak with you regarding our conversation intelligence and sales coaching platform, Refract. We're working with similar companies in your space. Give me a call back, I'd love to speak with you."*

*"Morning [Name], Mark Ackers from Refract. As I understand it you're the sales director at [company] and I wanted to discuss with you how our sales coaching platform is being used by similar companies to get 25% increase on their bottom line. Call me back on 07805410197, that's 07805410197 or email me at mark@refract.ai, thanks, Mark."*

Both are what I'd call standard voicemails and they both suck for similar reasons. The key theme with both is it's all about the sales rep and their company. It's what they want; why the prospect should listen; a mini pitch; and a list of happy clients. The prospect will be thinking "so what?" And who can blame them?

I also see no reason for reps, particularly when calling mobile phones, to read out their number. The prospect will be able to see the caller ID and will have the option to hit the call back button.

Voicemails need to stick with the principle of talking to your prospect about them, their problems, and their world. And they shouldn't give the prospect "a job". In this case, asking them to call you back is a job for them. If you've read and got comfortable with our take on cold calling, then leaving effective voicemails is going to come really easy for you as it follows many of the same principles.

# Your winning voicemail framework

Here's the blueprint for an effective voicemail that takes approximately 20 seconds to leave:

### The 20 second voicemail

*"Hey Kevin, read/ saw/ liked something you did/wrote – fantastic/ brilliant/ ingenious. Anyway, I've got a couple of new ideas that might not be on your radar, related to*

*[insert what they will care about top level]' specifically around [insert the end result of what they care about]. Kevin, no need to call me back, check your inbox for the ideas, and, oh, by the way this is Mark. All the best."*

So, if I was to call a Contact Centre Sales Director called Jenny, I might leave the following voice message:

*"Hey Jenny, just read your blog on sales kick offs – that idea you had re; roleplay is ingenious. Anyway, I've got a couple of new ideas that might not be on your radar, they're related to 'how tech can help you instantly improve the outcomes of your teams sales conversations' specifically around improving upselling and cross selling results. Jenny, no need to call me back, check your inbox for the ideas, and oh by the way this is Mark. All the best.*

I will then send her a short, to the point email, with a little more info on the ideas I've hinted at, and see if she'd be interested in talking further.

Let's break down why this 20 second voicemail works…

*"Hey Jenny, just read your blog on sales kick offs – that idea you had re; roleplay is ingenious".*

As ever, we start off with their favourite topic: them!

We didn't start with *"Hey my name is Mark with Refract"*. That's not as interesting to them in comparison to something personalised about what they have written, and the compliment you give ("ingenious") is like a mini dopamine shot. When you give people a genuine compliment like engaging with and liking their posts, it makes them instantly feel good and it will get their attention.

*"I've got a couple of new ideas that might not be on your radar…"*

This is transitioning from the relevance segment to sharing new ideas. We're not giving them the ideas, we're just teasing it. It's a bit like what happens at the end of a Netflix show: you get the cliffhanger that gives you a little tease of the next episode and you want to stay up and watch another.

The new ideas are then related to the things they care about and things that will make them better or happier in their role.

*"…no need to call me back, check your inbox for the ideas."*

Never give your prospects jobs to do. We therefore don't ask the prospect to call us back, because they probably won't. Instead we're promoting the next touch, which in this case is the email!

In the email subject line, use emotional words like "catapult" or "amplify and accelerate" and then relate it back to the end result of what they care about.

Subsequently, when they open the email, they'll see the ideas you have for them along with a promotion for the next touch point, which may be an introductory call.

**Two Top Tips**

**1:** Ahead of the voicemail, if you do find content you're going to reference, make sure you engage with it first. Or better yet, leave a thoughtful comment on it. Give them a follow on LinkedIn too. After all, you've found the content (the leg work). This last bit is taking it to the next level, as it gives you another opportunity to build familiarity with them. In addition, you're building engagement with your LinkedIn network.

What if you can't find any content? Try their company. Check out their corporate LinkedIn page, Twitter, Newsletter, Blogs, BBC news…

Still no luck? Try and find a "same here" opportunity.

A "same here" opportunity is when you can say to them you have something in common. People like people who share things in common.

*"Noticed you're in SaaS Sales – same here."*

*"Noticed you support Man United – same here."*

*"I can see your background was in recruitment, me too."*

*"I noticed you went to Newcastle University, same here."*

*"Notice you love to play golf, me too."*

**2:** Voicemails mobile-to-mobile get much higher listen rates. If you're going to leave a voicemail, call from your mobile phone.

# Voicemail Pitfalls

Here's a checklist of the biggest mistakes you can make when leaving a voicemail:

- Too long.
- Tone.
- Pitch.
- Too much information.
- Leaving too many for the same prospect.

## Too Long

Keep them as short as possible. The longer the voicemail (particularly if it's boring) the less they will listen to it. If they notice that this is a cold call voicemail and it's not piqued their interest, they're hanging up and deleting it.

## Tone

Inject personality. This isn't a two-way conversation and so you therefore have to have the right tone. Be enthusiastic about leaving them a message, particularly when referencing something they've done. That opening compliment/acknowledgment is vital, and if you sound dull they won't believe you.

Don't go the other way though. If you are *too* over the top, their bullshit detectors will go off.

**Pitch**

Never pitch. Think about it: when you pitch, people have thoughts, opinions and objections but at this stage you can't answer them. If they hear you pitch they could easily think "we already do this", "this isn't for us", "I'm not the right person" and so forth. Talk about problems and, if they have them, they will naturally be engaged. if they don't have those problems, then they're not for you anyhow.

**Too much Information**

At this stage, they don't need your number (especially twice!). They don't need to know who you work with. They don't need to know your job title or any "funky" Marketing/ROI stats.

As with pitching, the more you give, the more likely they are to think it's not for them.

Look back at the 20-second voicemail framework. We hardly give anything away yet we create interest and intrigue.

## Leaving too many for the same prospect

This is a balancing act, and there's no definitive right answer. But in my opinion, you can leave too many voicemails, just as you can send too many emails.

You should always leave a voicemail at the first time of calling and from there, pick and choose when you leave one and mix it up with other approaches such as LinkedIn, email, text etc. Check out Chapter Nine for more guidance on creating your prospecting cadence.

# Chapter Seven

# The Objection Handling Playbook

**Why we get objections**

There are many reasons why a prospect will give us an objection. Some are genuine, but some are not, meaning they're just trying to get rid of you. Sometimes, genuine prospects like to enter into a little objection duel to test you and see how good you are. Guilty as charged. I often do this and you should try it too, to see if anyone has some objection handling tips you can steal. Just don't be a dick about it.

Like anything, prevention is better than cure, and if you follow the instructions we've provided up to this point, you'll find the number of objections you receive is dramatically reduced. However, you'll never eradicate them as some are unavoidable. So it's crucial to be prepared to handle them.

So what's the main reason we get an objection?

The main reason we get objections is because we screwed up. We didn't do our job properly. Yes, you read that right. Objections are our fault!

An example would be where we didn't do a good enough job of leading with problems, and getting the prospect excited enough to want to hear more. They'll throw us an objection because we haven't got them eager to hear more. Our fault.

As humans, we are naturally uncomfortable with confrontation, so rather than simply saying "I'm not interested", most prospects will try to be nice and give an objection to save themselves an uncomfortable confrontation, but still get you off the phone.

## How to deal with them: embrace and ask questions

Let's work through a process to help you handle any objection that gets thrown your way. Objections strike fear into every salesperson, and the natural response is to become defensive and to start to tell the prospect how wrong they are and how brilliant your product is. Stop!

Don't get defensive, and don't enter into an argument. It's a lose-lose situation. I know we've been taught that salespeople need to overcome objections, but we also need to avoid battling with prospects. When you start trying to change your prospect's minds, and prove them wrong, you create resistance, and come across as a typical salesperson: one who is only interested in making as much commission as possible.

We need to be different. We're here to help our prospects solve problems, not sell them something they don't need and disappear as soon as the ink is dry on the contract. Selling is helping. If they don't have problems we can help with, then it's perfectly fine to walk away. You don't see doctors throwing prescription drugs at everyone, do you?

Instead, next time you get an objection, do nothing. Yes, you read that right. Take a second and breathe, before you jump in and reply. Count to three or five, and get comfortable with the silence.

When you do speak next, you want to acknowledge the objection, and make it clear that you've heard what your prospect is *really* saying. Everyone wants to feel like they've been heard, so make sure you show you've been listening.

After acknowledgment comes curiosity:

*"Help me understand – is this the only thing that concerns you? Because some of our best customers had a similar concern when we first spoke."*

Next, we want a response which will differ from objection to objection. Fear not, we've got most of the classic objections covered below, to give you step-by-step guidance on how best to respond, based on what you hear.

## Classic objections and the best responses

### *"No budget"*

I love this objection. It's such an easy one to overcome, especially if it's during a cold call. The reality is, there could be a number of reasons why the prospect is giving this objection:

1.    The company is in financial disarray, laying off employees, and heading for insolvency. Perhaps they aren't a good prospect right now?

2.     Spending is tight so they are being selective about what they invest in. But this doesn't mean they don't have any money to spend on the right products/services.

3.     It's a brush off. They are using this to get you off the phone as you haven't done a good enough job at positioning the value of your product/service.

Here's how I'd respond to options two and three:

*"Totally understand. Not having a budget could certainly be an issue but at this stage there are no big decisions Mr Prospect. I'm simply trying to determine if we're a good fit or not. A lot of our best customers invested in Refract without ever having a budget and yet when they saw the ROI we could provide, it was a no-brainer."*

*"You mentioned X is a problem for you. What I would suggest is we schedule some time to explore how we're solving this issue first, then once we've established if we can help or not, we can discuss budgets? Sound fair?'"*

Why does this work? Firstly, we confirm we've heard the customer and agreed with them that budget is important. We haven't tried to overcome it, or worse, argue how wrong they are by throwing every feature and benefit at them.

Next we disarm the objection. By stating that there are "no big decisions here", we're simply trying to find out if we can help or not. We're not asking them to buy, right here right now. Remember the purpose of the cold call? To get more of your prospect's time, and not to sell to them. This puts the prospect at ease as does the offer "to determine if we're a good fit or not." The crucial two words here are "or not". It gives the prospect a way out, and they aren't having to make any big decisions.

Next, we suggest that "a lot of our best customers never had a budget." This makes the prospect's concerns sound totally reasonable, but also reassures them that it isn't an issue. In fact, quite the opposite – we reassure the prospect that some of our best customers thought the same. It subconsciously plants the seed that they too could become one of our next best customers.

Finally, we respond by revisiting the problem they want to solve. We then take control of the conversation and suggest next steps with a reason.

As we know, when we make an ask, we always need a reason. Many studies have proven that the likelihood of a positive outcome significantly increases when you give a reason.

### "Not interested"

Many moons ago when I was a young lad, an old manager taught me to respond to this objection with the following script word for word:

*"'What are you not interested in? I haven't told you everything we do yet!"*

Can you imagine the responses from prospects? It wasn't pretty.

We know better than this now, and as we already know the first step to handling an objection is to relax, breathe, and not get defensive.

It's much harder to get this objection when you've led with problems. If a prospect has just agreed X is a problem for them, then it's very difficult for them to then say they aren't interested.

118

However, we will still sometimes get this objection. So we need to formulate a response, which looks a bit like this:

*"That's not an issue, Mr Prospect. Not being interested at this stage is totally understandable. I'm not sure we're a good fit yet either, but given you said X is a challenge for you, do you think it would be a good use of time for both of us to continue the conversation and explore if we are a good fit or not?*

*"Have you got 30 minutes for a call this afternoon or tomorrow?"*

Easy as that. Simple but effective.

**"We already do this"**

Same rules apply as always. What we need to do in this situation is to find out more.

*"That's awesome. I'm really pleased you've already invested in this type of technology/product/solution: could you talk me through how you do this today?"*

There are a few different paths the conversation can take at this stage:

- The prospect may be mistaken and not actually have a solution in place for this.
- They may be with a competitor.
- They do have a solution but what you offer could be much better.

If you find out they are working with a competitor then if they are stuck in a contract, don't waste your time. Thank them for taking your call, ask when the renewal date is and, if you really want to be an A-Player, ask if they could refer you to anyone else in their network who has similar challenges but hasn't got a solution in place yet.

Most won't have a solution in place and will still be facing problems. Once you've established this, it's easy to turn the conversation back to how you're different and how you solve the challenges they have. Now get your calendar open and book that discovery call to dive deeper.

*"No time"*

This is the classic cold call objection:

*"Sorry, I've not got time for this call, I'm just about to go into a meeting."*

First of all, we have to acknowledge it's probably true. Nobody has a free slot in their calendar marked "take cold calls" but that doesn't mean they don't have a couple of minutes to hear you out. It's normally just a defence mechanism, a knee jerk reaction to hearing a cold call.

*"I don't have time"/"I'm just going into a meeting"* normally comes after the pattern interrupt. So let's imagine you've asked for 35 seconds or similar and they hit you with *"Look, I'm really busy, I've not got time for this"*, you can go back with the following:

*"Yeah, sounds like you're busy, I'll be super quick."*

This casual, conversational style tells your prospect that you've heard them, you've acknowledged their concern and you'll make it snappy. Very rarely do they push back and that's because you've taken back control: from here you continue as normal.

You can also try:

*"Sure, I appreciate I've called out of the blue. If I was to say to you we help people solve the following problem(s) would that be worth us talking about at a more convenient time?"*

Again, this tells your prospect you've heard and understood them, and it's always important that the other person feels heard.

This reply teases them. If you're leading with the right problems, it will pique their interest and, more often than not, more time will magically appear or they will agree to a more suitable time to speak.

Here's another reply you can try:

*"Are you sure you don't want to take this call?"*

This is more direct. Perhaps some of you won't feel comfortable with it but here's why it can work. It challenges their mindset so that they have to wonder whether they really are sure. That moment of self-doubt and the curiosity you're stroking, will more often than not get the better of them.

*"How much does it cost?"*

This is one of the most frustrating questions you can get on a cold call because, the truth is, no matter what you say, it'll sound expensive. There's been little to no value identified at this point of the conversation, and two minutes ago they'd never even heard of you.

When this happens to me, (and it is rare I get this objection in a cold call) I acknowledge and answer them but do so at a high level and give them indicative costs. In my opinion, the alternative of avoiding or not answering the question just raises barriers, and creates tension and trust issues.

I'd typically reply with something like this:

*"Pricing is unique for each client as it's based on their specific requirements, which we're yet to discuss, and the number of users too.*

*We will cover pricing fully in our next call when I know exactly what you need but, for now, with the little understanding we both have at this early, exploratory stage, if I was to say to you ballpark costs are X would that kill our conversation?"*

Signing off with "would this kill our conversation?" is very final and forces your prospect to consider whether it really is the last time they want to talk to you.

The worst thing you can do is make this more of a conversation than it needs to be. Just reply, making it clear that this is an early stage conversation, and then move on.

There is an upside too. If you have touched on how you could solve potential pain points and you deliver your indicative costs in the right way, expectations around costs are managed ahead of the next call.

*"Send me some information"*

This is probably the easiest objection to overcome. People who give this objection usually sit in one of two buckets:

**Bucket 1:** They just want you off the phone, and whatever you send will never be read (this is the most common reason).

**Bucket 2:** Occasionally they will ask this as they simply don't understand what you've just said, but they heard something of interest and feel it would be easier to read about it than continue speaking with you.

Both buckets aren't great. But the key is to work out which bucket they are in.

If they're in bucket one, save yourself the effort of sending over a PDF.

If they're in bucket two, you can recover from this and still book the next step.

How do you work out which they are? Ask questions, and remember that they're asking you for something, so you can ask back. The biggest mistake a rep can make here is to surrender control and send over some collateral.

I pretty much <u>never</u> send any information either way. There is however one exception – when I've cocked up the call and this is my last chance at redemption.

Typically I'll say the following:

*"The truth is Mr Prospect I could send you a truckload of content but you don't want that in your inbox: nobody does.*

*Why don't we set up a call, we can continue the conversation in more detail, and I can share some ideas that might not be on your radar around problems XYZ. If at that point I feel I've got some relevant information to send over I can, does that sound fair to you?"*

If they're a bucket two you will then typically book in the next step as what you're suggesting is fair. If they're still resistant, then they're likely to be a bucket one. You'll know this for sure if they offer you an "info @ email address" or refuse to agree a time and date to speak with you again. I have, many times, when offered a generic email or resistance to booking in the next call just said:

*"Can I be honest, when I get info@ address/resistance to the next call, that's typically polite code language for 'I'm not interested': is this what's happening here?"*

Bucket twos will qualify back in here, explaining why that's not the right assumption. Now that you have regained control,you can take a second swing at suggesting the next call.

If, however, they agree with you and allow that it is a polite way of getting rid of you, take it as a win. You've qualified them out and saved a whole load of time. They will think more of you as well. My recommendation at this point is to say:

*"Let's not make this call a complete waste of time. Why don't we at the very least connect on LinkedIn, I have a strong network of [insert their profession here] and I often share content you may find valuable."*

They will always agree: you've at least grown your network, and if you're writing content for them, they may revisit you in the future.

If you do find yourself sending over some information to the prospect, make sure you agree on a time for a follow-up call as a next step:

*"Okay, Mr Prospect if I send over some case studies this afternoon, when would be a good time for me to give you a call to discuss this further?'*

If they're not willing to agree to even this next step, then maybe they simply aren't a good prospect for you right now.

**"I'm not the right person"**

Key to dealing with this objection is to understand why the prospect may believe they aren't the right person for you to be speaking with. I've consolidated these down to the following possibilities:

1.      They are genuinely not the right person.
If the prospect has a good understanding of what it is you do, then it may well be that they are not the best person to be dealing with. I personally quite like hearing this, as it's one of the easiest routes to getting a referral.

However, I would warn against simply asking *'Who should I be speaking with?'*

This approach may be met with resistance, and make the prospect reluctant to provide a colleague's name (in case they feel out of place doing so). I've found a better approach is asking the question:

*"Not sure who would be the best person to be speaking with here, but who do you suggest may be a good starting point for me to research?"*

Asking the question in this way makes it sound like you're going to do a lot of the leg work yourself, and by "researching" ahead of time. This gives the person on the phone the confidence that you're going to make an informed decision.

2.     They are the right person, but they just don't understand what you do.

We often have a high degree of confidence that the person we are speaking to is absolutely the right person. In this case, they've just misunderstood what it is you do and so don't feel it's relevant. To deal with this, self-deprecation is one of the best tactics. In other words, put the blame on yourself, not the prospect:

*"I've probably done a hopeless job of explaining how we help customers..."*

Then seek to understand by clarifying with the prospect that one of their key responsibilities is linked with a problem you know you help solve:

*"Would improving call quality and conversions be something that you are personally focused on?"*

I've often found that asking this question results in the prospect agreeing, and then subsequently asking for further clarity on what it is you do.

3. They are the right person, but feel they don't have the authority to make a decision.

"Not the right person" can often translate as "I'm a relevant person to be speaking with, but I don't make the final decisions on these things."

In scenarios like this, it's important to embrace this situation, make the prospect feel special, and see it as an opportunity to either gain information or build a champion. You will typically hear this response from someone who would be a key user of your product/service, but would not necessarily be the person who would sign a contract. They may feel nervous getting themselves involved in a purchasing decision, when they don't have the seniority to do so. In any case, it's probably going to be important to have these people involved in the buying cycle, as they will probably be a heavy influencer.

In this case, try this approach out:

Firstly, lower resistance and build assurance:

*"I totally understand that, and I'm not expecting you to make any purchasing decisions here. I was hoping to just*

*see at this point, if this could even be relevant to you or your company...."*

From here, the key is to get the prospect focused back on the problem you solve, and engaged in a conversation. Remember, the objective of the call is not to book a meeting. It's simply to find people who have a problem you might be able to solve:

*"Curious – would helping your SDRs have better outcomes in their sales calls be something you'd have a vested interest in?"*

**"Call back later"**

If someone asks you to call back later it is usually the response of somebody who simply wants to get you off the phone. I've typically found that the best way to decipher whether you have caught this person at a genuinely bad time or not is to consider the tone of their voice.

Do they sound like someone genuinely stressed and caught up in something? If so, then the worst thing you can do is ignore them and piss them off. Acknowledge the request, ask if they are free at a specific time later that day (being specific, for instance *"Can I catch you at 2:00pm?"* This gets them to focus on their calendar, in a way that *"Are you free this afternoon?"* doesn't). Either way, just accept that prospecting and catching people at the right time may require a number of attempts.

If you feel by the tone of their voice that you may still have a short window to speak with them there and then, a nice "up-front contract" is a great way of getting the prospect to feel comfortable that they can hear you out, but still have the option of saying "No".

*"Fully appreciate this may not be a great time. Give me literally 35 seconds to explain the reason I called and if you don't think it's worth your time, you can hang up on me. Fair?"*

These "mini up-front contracts" are great techniques for reducing sales resistance, as they serve as a constant message to the prospect that they have a way out if they want one.

### *"We're working with a competitor"*

This can be one of the most deflating things to hear from an ideal prospect once they have answered the phone. You've gone to all that effort and finally got

them on the other end of the line and then BAM!...
they are already in bed with one of your competitors.

I learned over time that this was actually quite a good
thing to hear from a prospect. Firstly, it indicates that
they already see value in your type of
product/service. Secondly, it gives you the perfect
opportunity to gain valuable information about
people you compete with and, importantly, your
prospect's opinion of working with them.

Some great follow-up questions to ask here include:

*"How long have you been working with them for?"*

This gives you a measure of how long and strong the
relationship is, and whether a renewal is on the
horizon (creating a great opportunity for prospects to
re-evaluate who they are working with).

*"What were some of the key problems you were hoping to
solve by working with them?"*

This allows your prospects to ultimately sell your
product to you, by giving you their reason or reasons
for buying in the first place.

*"Anything you feel could be improved?"*

This can be a compelling question which may reveal a specific area where your competitor is falling short, or perhaps not delivering a great experience.

The key here is not to trash-talk your competitors. It's not going to make you seem like an authentic or pleasant salesperson. And be perfectly comfortable and content if the prospect is completely happy with your competitor and there is no opportunity to influence them right now. Not everyone is a good prospect for you. In these situations, increase your perceived value with the prospect so they become more aware of you and your company. Invite them to an informative webinar, ask them if they'd be open to you sharing some interesting content with them, or connect on LinkedIn and use your personal brand to become more front of mind. Be helpful.

# Chapter Eight

# How to Write Killer Emails That Get Responses

As part of your prospecting activity it's important to use email as an alternative method of breaking through to your ideal contacts. In the following chapter, we will break down the key principles, composition and tactics of effective outbound emails as well as some great examples to help you get started.

## Composition of effective emails

### Length

There's lots of debate about how long an email should be. The de-facto opinion here is that prospecting emails should be as short as possible. In fact, Sales Engagement company SalesLoft claim that emails which are 50 words or less boost reply rates by 40%. The rationales for having shorter emails include:

- Prospects have short attention spans so they don't have time to read lengthy emails.
- Many prospects are reading cold emails on their smartphones. Any more than two or three swipes down the screen, and they are likely to get bored.
- Emails should get to the point quickly. They shouldn't be a long product pitch.

In spite of this, getting TOO obsessed about creating a really short email is not always healthy. I've written plenty of emails which are 200+ words long and achieved positive responses. The key is to make sure the message is both personalised and relevant (without turning it into an essay). If your email copy is compelling and personalised enough, prospects will read it. If you want a rule of thumb though, try and keep them under five sentences in length. A good practice is to read it back on your smartphone before sending it, to ensure you don't need to scroll too much when reading it.

**Structure**

My model for successful email composition, is to work in seven segments: The Subject Line, The

Salutation, The Opening; The Bridge; The Value Proposition; The Call to Action; The Power of the P.S.

I will break each of these down using real example emails I have personally sent and had positive responses to.

**The subject line**

The *only* objective of the subject line is to get the prospect to want to open the email. That's it.

Many people get this wrong as they *believe* the subject line has to be in some way connected with the content of the email itself.

Think of the subject line as the tease to get the prospect to want to find out more, however make sure that the subject line is not misleading with zero relevance as to why you're getting in touch.

I've found the best plan is to build in an element of mystery. Examples of this include;

- Thanks, *prospect name*
- Your comments, *prospect name*

- Re; your LinkedIn post/ Blog Post/ Tweet, *prospect name*
- Were you aware of this, *prospect name*?

All of these subject lines will entice the prospect to open the email.

Sometimes, you have to take a bit of a risk if you want to stand out. Dare to be different. My favourite subject line was one I sent to a fan of *The Great British Bake Off*.

"I hope you haven't got a soggy bottom, Sarah!"

If you're not familiar with the show, a "soggy bottom" is a big no no in the baking world. As Sarah was a massive fan of the show, I knew this would get her attention.

The cardinal sin of a subject line is to reference your product or company. It will scream out to the prospect "THIS IS A SALES EMAIL" which is a surefire way of having your prospecting emails sent to trash.

## The salutation

Hi, Hey, Hello, Bonjour. You don't need to overthink the salutation. What is most comfortable for you? Go with that. You'll find endless amounts of data arguing for example that "Hi" performs 1.745353428% better than "Hey" but I don't buy into this too much. There are far more important parts of the email to spend time thinking about.

However, if I find on LinkedIn that someone speaks another language, like French, I'll often open with "Bonjour". Again this shows you've done your research: and you can also translate some of the subject line into that language if you wish.

## The opening

The opening of your email is a critical component in getting a prospect engaged and wanting to read on. Get this wrong, and prospects could be hitting "Delete" before they've reached the second sentence.

There are two big things to consider here: *personalisation* and *curiosity*.

Take a look at the email opening below, which was sent to a CEO of a £30m business: it resulted in me getting a positive response:

---

Phil

Came across a recent article about Love Energy Savings smashing through 10,000 Trustpilot reviews. It's great to see a company getting the rewards for delivering great sales experiences for their customers, but I also noticed one of your reviews highlighted your team's ability to cross-sell other utility savings to help customers.

---

By referencing a specific article which relates to the prospect's company, I've made the email "all about the prospect" straight out the gate. The prospect knows this email was intended for him, and is likely not to have been sent to hundreds of others. This personalisation is key to getting the prospect to recognise that this is not a "mass-blast" email. Key to personalisation is finding "trigger events" that relate to your prospect. This could be content they've posted on LinkedIn, recent company news, an industry event or something else. Ultimately, it has to be both relatable to the prospect AND relatable (in some way) to your company's value proposition.

In addition, I have created *curiosity* in the prospect by referencing a review which pointed to the fact his company also cross-sells other services to customers. He wants to read on!

**The bridge**

"The bridge" is the connection between the email opening and the value proposition, the real reason you have got in touch. Again, I want to ensure that I get the prospect hungry to keep reading, much like a great book leaves you wanting to keep turning the pages, or starting a new chapter.

> But what if you could identify every sales conversation where missed cross-sell opportunities are occurring, without having to listen to every call, and drive more revenue as a result?

I've found one of the most powerful ways of building on this curiosity is by making your bridge a question. The aim of the question is to make the prospect think about a problem they perhaps weren't previously tuned into, while getting them hungry to hear the solution. You will notice in the example above, that I've made the bridge relevant to the email opening by referencing "missed cross-sell opportunities". This is where understanding your customer is so crucial, as you need to ensure that the questions you are posing to the prospect are things which will correspond to a key problem or challenge they are likely to want to tackle. In my case, I know that it is likely that this CEO will want to solve the problem of too much money being left on the table by his sales team not cross-selling consistently, and the lost revenue as a result.

One mistake too many make with their cold emails is that their "bridge" bears no connection to their email opening. This confuses prospects, but also makes the email feel fake and unauthentic.

**The value proposition**

Another big mistake people make with their cold emails is the same problem they make with their cold calls. They turn them into product pitches. Remember, for the initial outreach the aim is simply to find people who may have a problem which you might be able to solve, and who want to talk more with you. Turning your email into a product pitch will often result in a prospect thinking "so what?", and not responding.

Key to any value proposition is to tease your prospects with a likely solution which you have hinted about in the bridge. The aim is to provoke your prospect into wanting to find out more and respond. Here's an example of how I've done this before with a different email:

---

Curious - what's stopping you from having a deeper understanding about what your competitors are doing here, and exploring some lesser known approaches to improving conversions of sales calls and demos, without the huge investment of listening to hours of call time?

---

In this example, I'm "provoking" the prospect by asking them "what's stopping you...?" and referencing competitors of theirs who are getting great results by working with us. Furthermore, I am ensuring that the value proposition is focused on the problem the prospect is likely to be facing. In this case, that is "improving conversions of sales calls and demos".

In order to craft a compelling value proposition, you MUST understand your customers and what problems "grind their gears". In addition, you need to portray those problems in their words... not in jargon-filled Marketing language. More on this in Chapter Fourteen.

**The call to action**

Key to signing off any outbound email is to make it easy for the prospect to respond. But let us remember that the objective of the cold email is the same as the cold call... simply to find prospects who have a problem you may be able to solve and who want to talk further.

Traditionally, many "calls to action" on cold emails end with the salesperson asking for a meeting or to speak at a certain time. Prospects have become tired of these requests over time, –so this method is now less effective than it once was. From a buyer's perspective, I can also empathise with the feeling that these requests sound too presumptuous from the seller, and perhaps over-demanding.

Below are some example alternative calls to actions I have leveraged and some analysis of each:

*The Sceptical Curiosity Ask:*

> Not even sure if it's a fit yet, but I've a couple ideas to share.
> Open to swapping a couple of messages and you can decide?

This approach is designed to come across as extremely "non-pushy" by having an almost sceptical tone. Telling the prospect that I'm not even sure whether my product makes sense for them makes the prospect feel comfortable that there is no hidden agenda here.

In addition, I ask the prospect whether they are simply open to exchanging a couple of messages so they can find out more and then THEY can decide what they want to do. I'm putting all of the power in the prospect's hands. Again, the objective here is simply to get a response and to find out if the prospect is open to talking.

146

*The "Would It Make Sense?" Ask:*

> Would it make sense to connect Douglas?
>
> Best,
>
> Rich

A great alternative to asking for a meeting on a cold email is simply to ask if it would make sense to connect. The phrase "make sense" implies a good logical approach. When things seem logical, they seem to be the right thing to do. In this regard, I'm asking the prospect whether connecting with me feels logical given the problems I've shone a light on in my value proposition.

*The "Get Out Option" Ask:*

> If you give me a shot this Thursday at 9:00am ET to share how other SaaS companies are reducing missed sales opportunities and increasing conversions using Refract, I promise we can part ways if you aren't impressed.

Ok, so perhaps this does slightly go against the grain of my advice to avoid calls to action directly asking for a follow-up call, but this approach does have a different dimension to it. As we saw in the section on making cold calls, an "up-front contract" is an effective approach as it gives prospects the freedom and option to say "no thanks". As such, it goes a long way to reducing sales resistance and getting prospects on side. In this example, the "Get Out Option" is telling the prospect that we can part ways, if they aren't impressed when we talk. Furthermore, the conversation I am proposing is simply "to share" how similar companies are reducing missed opportunities and getting better sales results. Who wouldn't want to pay attention to that?!

**The power of the P.S**

I remember a couple of years ago, someone on the Refract sales team started getting an abnormally high response rate to their cold emails. After analysing what they had started doing, we noticed that they had been adding in a "P.S" at the end of every email they had been sending, which was filled with additional personalisation. This typically had nothing to do with the main body of the email itself, but often just provided some further reassurance that this email was indeed meant for the recipient and the recipient only. Some of the most effective personalisation referred back to a specific interest the prospect had (often discovered from their social media accounts).

For example, I once discovered a prospect was a fan of the WWE wrestler Stone Cold Steve Austin. Check out the P.S I wrote for a him:

> Would it make sense for us to connect John?
>
> Rich
>
> P.S Any Stone Cold fan is a good guy in my eyes

In the next example, I discovered that the prospect I was emailing used to play professional football:

> Open to swapping a couple of messages and you can decide?
>
> Rich
>
> P.S Noticed you used to play third division football in Scotland. Do you miss those days? Stark contrast to FinTech!

The P.S is not just effective because it provides some additional personalisation: it also helps inject some much needed personality into the equation, and makes you appear more human (which people warm to). Don't take my word for it, give it a try and see your response rates rocket!

## The Refract email script

Do you want to start writing your own emails? Here's the formula we use at Refract, which you can easily adapt and use as your own:

### Opening line

*Thanks for sharing/I read your* [insert article name, tweet, or comments etc]. *I totally agree* [insert piece of info from their LinkedIn, blog, tweet etc].

*As you rightly said* [insert another piece of personalisation from their LinkedIn, blog, tweet etc] Here's a real example:

> Thanks for sharing your article "SDR to AE: Prepping for Draft Day", I couldn't agree more with the parallels between coaching a top college sports team, and coaching a high producing Sales Development team.

## The bridge

This is the hard part: we need to link from the end of your personalization to the reason for the email. Get this right and the email will be a winner: get it wrong and it can sound a bit disingenuous.

Here's the example I used with the above email:

> How is tribal knowledge shared among your three remote teams, Steve?

Why does this work? More personalisation – "three remote teams" and starting to mention a challenge we help with here at Refract. Boom! We're halfway there and this email is starting to take shape.

**The value proposition**

Most of our value propositions are recycled based on the ICP and the company we are prospecting.

Remember to make it about your prospect and the problems you think they are facing based on similar clients you help.

Here's the value proposition I used in the above email:

*Remote teams have been using Refract to collaborate for years.*

Similar companies like ACME had frustrations regarding how long it took to get new hires up to speed and difficulty in bridging the gap in performance between A players and the rest of the team.

Next we have the ask. Now remember, as discussed above, the purpose of the email isn't to sell your product, it's to start a conversation. Here's what works well for us:

> Would you be open minded to me sharing a few ideas, all exploring how we may be able to help you and your team?

## Key email best practices

### It's not about you

The most common mistake I see eager reps making in their cold emails is talking all about themselves and their company. Like everything in sales... IT'S NOT ABOUT YOU!

The sooner you understand that the better. Here are three things you can do today before hitting send on your email, that will dramatically improve your response rates:

- Read the email back and check for spelling and grammar mistakes (use 'Grammarly' to help as it's free).

- Remove as many "I"s or mentions of your company and product as you can. Remember – it's not about you.
- Get really critical of any language that isn't 100% essential to the email and remove it. The shorter the email the better. There's certain things you obviously need to include, but get rid of everything else and get to the point.

Bonus tip – Send the email to yourself and view it on your mobile device. Ideally you should be able to view the entire email without scrolling. You also want that killer PS to be visible at first glance.

**Good times to send an email**

Try not to overthink this. We've shown a slightly higher response rate between 8-9am (in the prospect's time zone) or between 5-6pm, but the difference is negligible. As long as you're not sending the email in the middle of the night, I wouldn't worry too much.

Bonus tip – When using scheduling tools, don't use the default time which is normally set to sending on the hour or 15 minutes past. Avoid this, and pick a random time as most will be sending the emails at the default times. You have to be different to everyone else.

**Personalisation (research)**

I've mentioned personalisation a lot, and there is a good reason for that. Here are the things we need to be looking out for, ordered with the most powerful first:

Self authored content: If they've written a blog, article, or a post on LinkedIn, this is golden material. We have an 80+% reply rate with this type of content.

You will typically find this content on LinkedIn, or if they have a blog on the company website. Always remember to Google your prospects name or company name. It's amazing what you'll find out about them.

Comments and Tweets: These are also great. Any comments they have made on LinkedIn or Tweets they have sent, can be used to personalise your email. For instance: "I read your comments on LinkedIn Steve, I totally agree......." Notice that the email starts to write itself.

Linkedin Profile/Company Bio: Mention things they say about themselves on their profile. An example would be "I'm a rockstar HR manager with a passion for heavy metal" or "I'm a Purchasing Manager who's obsessed with red wine." These are highly personal things, and when you mention them in your emails, the prospect knows you've created this email especially for them.

Hobbies/Interest: Twitter is a great source of this information, which can be used to create a great PS. LinkedIn also has a mention of interests, schools they attended, what sports they played etc.

What about a situation where you can't find any content at all?

You have two options here and an email probably isn't the answer. You have a much better chance of connecting by speaking with someone than by sending a generic cold email. If I find an ideal prospect who has no content, and we can't get through on the phone, I'll send them some content which is relevant for them in their role and company. Always bear in mind that the less personalisation you include, the lower your reply rate is going to be. So get digging for that info.

# Chapter Nine

# Your Prospecting Cadence

As we previously hinted, to be an effective prospector you need to have both process and rhythm. Sporadic prospecting and doing little bits "here and there", will rarely return consistent results. Moreover, follow-up in prospecting is key, and using a blend of approaches and methods is critical, as different prospects will typically respond better to some methods than others. In this chapter we will help you build a process into your prospecting activity and a simple framework to figure out what you need to put in to get the results you desire.

## Sequencing

A sequence, also referred to as a prospecting cadence, is a scheduled series of sales activities that can include emails, social messages, calls, connection requests, SMS and so on. Some even include flowers in the post! Any activity you'd use to reach out to a prospect can be included. The schedule means these tasks are delivered at a predetermined point in time over a number of days, weeks, or maybe even months. See Chapter Sixteen for more information on the platforms that enable you to create, deliver, and monitor your sequences.

Let's get this straight. Don't use this sequence to spam the life out of thousands of prospects. You're better than that.

But without process to your prospecting, then you're going to let good quality prospects fall through the cracks.

Check out a suggested sequence below. It's a process that we use, which has been tried, tested, and tweaked more times than I care to remember. It works very, very well:

**Day 1**
Touch 1 – Follow them on LinkedIn
Touch 2 – Cold call
Touch 3 – Leave a voicemail
Touch 4 – Send email one

**Day 4**

Touch 5 – LinkedIn connection request. If they accept, revert to LinkedIn sell-by-chat (see 'sell-by-chat' later in this chapter)

Touch 6 – Call (don't leave a voicemail)

Touch 7 – Send email two

**Day 8**

Touch 8 – Cold call

Touch 9 – Send email three

**Day 12**

Touch 10 – Cold call

Touch 11 – Send email four

**Day 15**

Touch 12 – Cold call

Touch 13 – Break up email

Every time I discuss sequences, everyone wants to know what email copy we use. The truth is that it's different for every ICP, but I've lifted some of the most popular emails. Feel free to steal, tweak, and use as your own.

**Email one**

I can't stress this enough. This email needs to be as personalised as possible. This is not a generic email that can be sent to 100 prospects at a time.

Top Tip: Before hitting send, imagine being your prospect and read the email back with that in mind. Your email must read as though it was written specifically for them, and it couldn't possibly have been sent to anyone else.

The latest example from my inbox at the time of writing is below:

---

Hi Gino,

Great post - I totally agree 'BANT' is for Active Opportunities, it's not a Sales Dev measurement.

If the SDR has got the Decision Maker at a target company to take the call, their job is done and the rest is down to the AE.

Not sure if we're a good fit or not yet Gino, but are you open to finding out how we're helping other Sales Development Leaders find out the mystery across all of their team's conversations in seconds versus hours?

Are you free for a call Thursday or Friday this week to share a few ideas?

Thanks,
Stuart

P.S Absolutely love the idea of "Whine Wednesday"

---

A personal email does take time, but it is time well spent. This email, combined with the rest of the steps in Day one gets us a 73% response rate. Check out

Chapter Eight for more inspiration on writing killer emails.

**Email two**

The brilliance of email two is its simplicity. It's just two little words:

> "Any thoughts?"

That's it. No "hello". No "thanks" or "kind regards". Just those two words.

Try it for yourself.

**Email three.**

This email does change depending on your ICP, but here's an example:

> Hi Leanne,
>
> Things can get buried in busy inboxes. Keen to share a couple of ideas about how we're helping similar companies [solve key problem].
>
> Would it be ridiculous to schedule a brief call tomorrow or the next day?
>
> Thanks,
>
> Stu

## Email four

This one is last but not least. You'll notice we're quite light on the number of emails in our sequence, but we have thirteen touches in fifteen days, and we've tested so many different options. This is currently our most successful sequence:

Hi Leanne,

Unfortunately, we haven't been able to connect yet. Totally understand; life gets busy.

Still really confident we can help you solve [insert problem], if that's something you're bumping into?

Are you open to a brief conversation so I can share how we might be able to solve this? How about tomorrow morning or Wednesday afternoon?

Thanks,

Stu

That's it. It looks simple on paper and I guess it is. There's no magic formula. If you tweak it to make it your own it'll yield huge success as it does for us. Remember. It works best when combined with a multichannel approach, so don't hide behind emails and avoid the cold calling aspect as laid out above.

## The maths of prospecting: know your numbers.

At the end of the previous section, we discussed focusing on what you can control and trying to forget the rest. This is arguably a recipe for success not only in sales, but life in general.

The older I get the less I care what other people think of me and that's given me greater freedom to do the things I want to do.

There's an age-old debate as to whether sales is a science or art, which I'm not going to get into here. What I will say is that in order to be a successful prospector you need to know your numbers, and maths plays a big part.

Before you can start anything, you need to start tracking so you know where you are today:

- How many emails do I need to send in order to get a positive reply?
- How many dials does it take to speak with a prospect?
- How many prospects do I need to speak with in order to book a meeting?
- How many meetings take place?
- How many of those meetings turn into demos?
- How many demos will result in won business?
- What is my average order value?

If you can't answer the questions above, then start tracking these metrics and find out. Only then can you work out what you need to do in order to hit your number.

Let's imagine we need to achieve 20 meetings a month.

Firstly, you need to know how many prospects you must speak with on a monthly basis in order to book 20 meetings. If your outreach has a 4% success rate for booked meetings you know that in order to hit 20 meetings you need to prospect 500 contacts every month.

Now if you want to smash your target you have two options. Do you:

A: Contact more people

B: Try and improve the 4% conversion rate

Frankly, you'd be crazy not to try and do both.

Let's imagine we increase our productivity and performance by 20%... We start reaching out to 600 people a month instead of 500 and the positive response rate increases to 5% from 4%.

Doesn't sound a lot but we've now booked 30 meetings – 150% of target. Presidents' club and pay rise here we come!

Breaking down the sales process and looking at ways in which you can improve performance and productivity are massively important. Marginal gains are possible in every area of your sales process and when multiplied together they're a game-changer.

So this whole process starts with knowing your numbers: and until you know what they are, you haven't got a hope in hell of improving them.

Once I worked out my numbers, I had the formula for success and this enabled me to replicate similar performances with the rest of my team, thus making our prospecting far more predictable.

Knowing your numbers also makes it easier to diagnose problems. Poor prospecting performance often comes down to one of two things – lack of activity or poor quality messaging. For example, if your results have dropped one month and your activity is on point then you know you need to look at your messaging or vice versa.

# Chapter Ten

# Using LinkedIn to Drive More Conversations

One of the biggest changes in prospecting over the past decade has been the introduction and impact of social media when engaging with prospects. If you're not making full use of valuable tools such as LinkedIn, you're leaving money on the table.

## How your LinkedIn profile should look

Your LinkedIn profile is just that, it's yours. It's your identity and whether you like the phrase or not, it's your brand. From this online presence comes opinions, perceptions, and judgement from your prospects. SO, let's do what we can to make sure it's a positive one.

Your LinkedIn profile is one of the first things your buyers will look at, and the vast majority of the time they'll look at it before they respond to your email.

Don't be surprised if they are even looking at it during a cold call.

Not convinced?

Do you research your prospects on LinkedIn? You know that "who viewed your profile" feature? If you look at their profile, they might look at yours BEFORE you've had a chance to contact them, meaning your name and their perception of you, is already floating around in their mind and can influence whether they reply to your email or how receptive they might be to your cold call.

Reminder: many buyers may turn off the "who viewed your profile" feature, meaning you can't see if they've been on your profile. Outside of the sales profession, it's not uncommon for people to switch this feature off.

If you're in sales, your LinkedIn profile should be working for you. By that, I mean it should be helping you create awareness in your buyer's mind of the problems they may have and solutions you can provide. Your profile should help you build trust, confidence, and expertise in your subject area.

Your LinkedIn should NEVER be a CV, a bragging forum, or an empty canvas, like one with no profile photo or bio.

Here are the ways you can optimise your LinkedIn Page for your ICP:

- Professional photo
- Background image
- Headline
- About Section
- Featured
- Experience
- Recommendations
- Skills

**Professional Photo**

Keep it simple with a headshot against a plain background. Don't forget to smile!

Some choose to put photos that stand out, for instance by using bright colours or unusual backgrounds. Some choose to put a photo of them doing something they enjoy like riding a horse, and then there's also the classic "lads' "who like to show they can drink a beer or posh cocktail. Don't be that last one, whatever you do.

If you can get a professional headshot done, I would recommend it, but it's really not essential with the quality on modern camera phones. You can often find free headshots are taken at trade shows too.

**Background image**

This is your billboard. You can use this in a few ways but the goal is to reinforce you, your brand, and that you're credible. Suggestions include:

- Company logo, strapline and call to action
- Highlighted problems you solve
- You giving a talk or delivering a presentation

If you can, make one yourself. If you have a colleague who can help, ask them or pay someone to make one for you. Websites like Fiverr.com can hook you up with a designer who can make you one really cheap. It's worth investing in.

**Headline**

There are two schools of thought on this one:

1.     Put your job title, as people want to know what you do.

2.     Put something creative that explains what you do or why they should be interested

I originally went with number two, until I wondered whether, now that everyone had something "quirky" in their headline, I was really standing out. So I switched back to number one. I also feel that job titles can have weight, and if you're in a "leadership" position for example, you're more likely to be taken seriously than if you are in a junior role.

Think about it: if you're a Sales Director and you prospect fellow Sales Directors, they're more likely to see you as their equal and sympathise with your situation. If you're a Sales Executive or an SDR reaching out to the same person, they're less likely to respond.

So I concluded that if you have a job title with "weight", you should keep your job title. If you're not in that position and reaching out to people that are, be creative. The one rule is that whatever you write must be concise enough to be readable in the "who viewed your profile" section. If your title is cut off half way, then what's the point?

Here are some examples of profiles that I feel have good profile pictures, background photos, and headlines:

Josh Braun · 1st [in]

Struggling to book meetings? Getting ghosted? Want to sell without selling your soul? Read this profile.

Boca Raton, Florida · 500+ connections · Contact info

Sales DNA

Florida State University

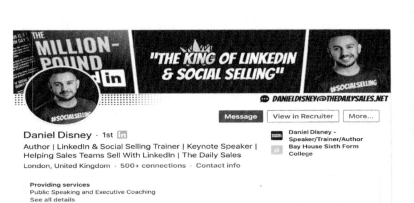

Daniel Disney · 1st [in]

Author | LinkedIn & Social Selling Trainer | Keynote Speaker | Helping Sales Teams Sell With LinkedIn | The Daily Sales

London, United Kingdom · 500+ connections · Contact info

Daniel Disney -
Speaker/Trainer/Author
Bay House Sixth Form
College

Providing services
Public Speaking and Executive Coaching
See all details

Message | View in Recruiter | More...

**Martin Middlehurst EISM** · 1st

New Business Manager at Northgate Vehicle Hire | UK's
largest B2B light commercial vehicle rental provider

Penrith, England, United Kingdom · 500+ connections ·
Contact info

Northgate Vehicle Hire

Edge Hill University

## About Section

Let me give you some examples of what a bad "About" section looks like:

- Blank space
- Talks about themselves
  - In the 3rd person
  - Bragging about achievements
  - Bullshit
- Talks about awards their company has won
- No call to action

Just because it says "About", it doesn't mean anyone wants to read specifically about you. If your prospects are viewing your profile, that means your

178

photo, background and headline has sparked some interest. Don't spoil it now by pitching, instead, make sure you lead with value. If someone wants to read your "About" section, it's because they want to know what it is about you that's relevant or helpful to them. Remember their favourite topic is themselves, and so make sure you appeal to it. Make it easy for them, don't give them a job to do, and don't make it hard for them to figure out why they should want to continue reading and ultimately to speak with you.

**Blank Space**

Nobody would swipe right on a Tinder profile with no picture or bio. Why would your prospects read on if you had a blank "About" section or no photo?

**Self-Promotion: Avoid!**

As we said, at this stage, they don't want to read about you specifically as a person. They're reading because they're curious to see if what you do is relevant to them.

Bonus cringe points if you talk about yourself in the third person.

The worst thing you can do though is brag or bullshit. Think about it, nobody wants to buy from a "quota crushing" sales rep. Who wants to speak to someone who shows off about their strong negotiation skills or similar?

As for bullshitting, people can see through inauthentic, false, and clickbait-style posts. It just comes across as disingenuous and damages their perception of you.

**Company Awards**

I see the argument that mentioning these "builds credibility". However, the reality is that at this stage, nobody cares about the awards you've won and they tend to mean very little in today's world in any case. Awards can often be won by an event sponsor, or given out by another company.

If you have a genuine, credible award then a subtle nod is fine.

**No Call to Action**

They've gotten to the end of your "About' section", so why wouldn't you give them your details?

# A Good "About" Section

## Below are some examples of strong "About" sections:

### About

Do you work with sales reps, coaching them to have better, more successful cold calls, discovery calls, demos and/or face to face meetings?

Do you find yourself frustrated, that so much of your revenue comes from a disproportionate number of reps in your team, i.e your 'top performers'?

Do you lack true visibility into why some of your team's sales conversations are successful and others aren't?

Does it take you too long to onboard new hires and get them contributing to your team quota?

Sales Leaders have adopted our coaching platform to unlock the hidden value tucked away in their team's sales conversations, our tech and AI insights provides instant clarity into what makes your top performers more successful and enables you to coach your entire team have better, more effective conversations with their prospects.

## 'Featured'

This is where you can 'feature' your best content. This might include posts, articles, links, or other media.

Use this section to profile the content your ICP is going to get the most value from. Ask yourself what content you would like them to see that would grab their attention.

Don't just feature content that you like the most or that has the most engagement. Instead, use it to feature content that sells what you do without you doing the selling.

Below is what a good "Featured" section looks like:

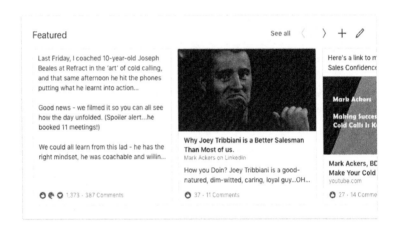

The two main posts you can see are carefully selected. The first is a post that shows how using Refract's technology helped to coach a 10-year-old to make a cold call. This is a post that not only performed really well, but captured the attention and imagination of our ICP. This content can then be shared with as many people as possible, because not only does it subtly showcase the problems Refract solves, but also piques interest into how it works.

The second is a blog that hasn't performed *that* well, but Joey Tribbiani's face and linking him to sales will get clicks. The post again subtly refers to Refract and looks to grab the attention of our ICP.

If you're not currently writing any content, you should be. More on this later.

**Experience**

This is a mini version of the "About" section: however you don't need to actually list your experience. Instead, use it as a supporting piece of content.

Top tip: all you want your viewer to read is your current role, right? You don't want them to get distracted with where you've previously worked and what you did there. It's just noise. Only keep your job title, the company name, and your dates of employment.

## Recommendations

Ask for them. Get your happiest and most successful customers, former colleagues and so on to give you recommendations. They help you add credibility and improve people's perception of your brand.

Not having them is a wasted opportunity.

Try and get them specifically from your ICPs if possible. You just need to ask.

## Skills

I've personally never embraced the "Skills" section as it feels a bit too "easy" for me (and a bit too "tick box"). They mean very little and I can't say I ever pay them any attention when landing on another profile.

If however you're just starting to beef out your profile, this is a fast way to build some credibility. Add in the skills you think your ideal prospects will care most about. Again, try to avoid the bragging ones like negotiation, sales and so on, as your buyers don't want to see that. Instead, add skills that will suggest to your prospects you're an expert in their field and you have the credibility to help them.

## Sell-by-chat

This is a new method of prospecting we've implemented in the last twelve months at Refract. It involves creating a casual conversation on LinkedIn to pique interest and schedule a call with your ideal prospect.

For this, I must give credit to one of our top performing SDR's at Refract, John Sutherland.

I'm a big fan of giving the team the autonomy to take chances and try new ideas. As a result, John came up with a new way of selling that we'd not considered. We call it sell-by-chat.

It's really simple but massively successful. John doubled his performance overnight and I'm going to share his approach step-by-step so you can do the same.

The beauty is in the simplicity as it sounds almost too good to be true. Almost...

Create a list of ideal prospects on LinkedIn SalesNav. You should be a whizz at this by now.

Create a personalised connection request that you can copy and paste. Something like:

*"Hi Dave,*

*From one sales professional to another it would be great to join your network.*

*Thanks,*

*Stu"*

Now, we wait.

Once the connection request is accepted, send the next message:

*"Can I ask you a couple of quick questions, Dave?"*

Wait for a reply. If they reply, then great. Get the conversation started and hit them with your questions.

If they don't reply within 24 hours, send a follow-up message like this:

*"May I go ahead and ask, Dave?'*

Currently, we're seeing over 50% response rate and most of them are happy to be hit with a quick question or two.

Now this is the crucial bit. Your questions need to be ultra-relevant but easy enough for them to reply to quickly. This is "sell-by-chat". We want back and forth but we don't want war and peace. Think how you communicate with friends and family on text or WhatsApp. That's the approach you're trying to replicate.

Question one:

*"Would you say there are moments in your sales team's calls where mistakes and missed opportunities are happening, Dave?"*

That's it. Lead with a problem your prospect likely has, and ask if it resonates with them or if it is something they're 'bumping into'.

The most common response we get is:

*"Yes, of course, every conversation will have mistakes and missed opportunities."*

Next, we go for the kill with question two:

*"How helpful would it be if you could automatically find not only every mistake and missed opportunity but also every moment of best practice your team demonstrates?"*

Again, the most common reply is :

*"Very helpful, how do you do it?"*

Now we've got them and our work here is almost done. Remember, just because they've asked you how you do it, resist the temptation to go into pitch mode. Here's what you reply back with:

*"What I'd suggest is we jump on a call Dave and I can share how we're helping similar companies like X, Y, and Z do exactly this? How are you fixed tomorrow at 10.30?"*

This is just one example of creating a conversation on LinkedIn and "selling-by-chat". This method works better than I would ever have imagined. It's very hot at the moment and yet to be abused by the masses, so we need to make hay while the sun shines.

As with anything, keep AB testing your approach to keep it fresh and performing as well as possible.

## LinkedIn Voice Messages

I'm calling this right now. LinkedIn voice messages are the most untapped and highest potential method of breaking through "the noise" that exists right now for the modern day prospector.

I remember the first time I heard about LinkedIn voice messages was when I was on the receiving end of one last year. Out of the blue, a sub-one minute audio file from a salesperson landed in my LinkedIn inbox.

Now I don't know about you, but there was absolutely no way I WASN'T hitting play on that media file. The curiosity part of my brain was telling me I needed to hit play and hear what was behind the mystery.

It's not like a cold email or LinkedIn mail which I can scan and visually understand the context of a message in a matter of seconds (and so can decide whether I want to read on or hit "delete"). A recorded voice message doesn't offer the same luxury.

And that is the beauty of LinkedIn voice messages. On top of this, there are other reasons why this new age prospecting method is so powerful:

- Voice messages give your prospects a really good feeling/insight to you – the person behind the message. Being able to hear the tonality, warmth, and authenticity of your voice builds that human connection far more than a written message can.
- Voice messages have a one minute limitation on them. It forces the sender to make them short and snappy, and encourages prospects to listen to the end.
- There aren't many people sending these. I can count on one hand the number I've received since these were launched. I've listened AND responded to every single one.

That being said, as with anything in sales – there's always a way to be effective and ineffective and my experience of LinkedIn voice messages is no different.

Here are some of the pitfalls you may want to avoid:

- Jumping into pitch mode straight away. As we've repeatedly said, slapping your prospects with a product pitch is a surefire way of having your voice message ignored.
- Not being crispy and specific enough with your message. Remember, you have a maximum of one minute to get your point across, and so a waffled or confusing message is not going to get you the response you are looking for.
- Forgetting to put a "call-to-action" at the end of your voice messages. I've heard some voice messages where I didn't really know what the salesperson wanted me to say or do in response.

Remember, much like all other prospecting methods, it is crucial to make your message personalised, relevant, and curiosity-provoking. LinkedIn voice messages are no different.

Here is a framework for effective voice messages to follow:

**Step One:** Increase the chances of having your voice messages played by starting with a line of text accompanying your voice message to entice the prospect to hit play. Below is a great example of this:

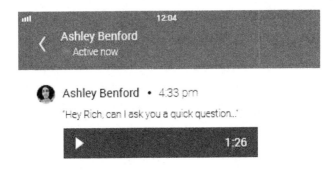

**Step Two:** Keep your first message short and snappy by leading with a question, potentially about a trigger event such as something they have posted or a piece of industry news which is relatable to the prospect. You need to capture the prospect's attention and engage them in a conversation. Remember, do not pitch your product.

*"Hey Rich, noticed your recent post about the hiring drive that you are embarking on. I'm going to assume you haven't thought about how you aim to onboard your new sales hires remotely yet?"*

**Step Three:** Once the prospect has responded to your LinkedIn voice message, they start to get into the habit of responding again and again. So once the prospect has responded to your initial question, send them a second message which asks them a second question. A good approach here would be to take the cold calling approach of "leading with problems". In this specific example, you could lead with two key problems your prospect might typically be facing when it comes to on-boarding new sales hires.

*"Typically when I speak with other VPs of Sales who are growing their team, they tell me that it's really difficult to onboard new hires remotely, whereas others are concerned about the time it takes to get a new hire ramped and generating revenue consistently. Which of those two things are you thinking about?"*

**Step Four:** Once you have got a prospect to tell you that they are thinking about a specific problem you could potentially help solve, use a combination of a "clue" (to the solution of the problem), and a "small-ask" which will get the prospect to commit to a time for a more in-depth conversation. You will find that because the prospect has got into the habit by responding to two or three voice messages, they will be more inclined to respond again.

*"If there was a solution to solving the challenge of ramping new hires in less time, would it be a ridiculous idea for us to have an exploratory phone call to see if there's something that we could potentially help with or not?"*

Remember, the key is to generate dialogue and conversation. Make your tone natural and not scripted. Practice by sending your friend or colleague voice messages before you drop one into your prospect's inbox.

n.b. LinkedIn voice messages are currently only available to use on the LinkedIn mobile app.

# Chapter Eleven
## Video Prospecting

Despite feeling like it has been around for some time now, video prospecting is still very much in its early adopter stage. Much like LinkedIn voice messages, the very fact that not many people are sending them means that if executed correctly, personalised video messages can be a great way to stand out from the crowd.

To further back this up, SalesLoft ran a study of 134 million emails, of which only 3.3% contained an embedded video. They found that when a video was included the average open rate increased by 16% and the average reply rate increased by 26%. Impressive stats!

The timing of sending a video message in your prospecting cadence is key. In the relatively small number I've sent out, I've found they are most effective with those prospects who have proven to be hard to reach, or who have opened, but not responded to an initial email. It's very much a case of finding the right approach for the right prospect.

**Best Practices:**

Here's a few things to consider when sending a prospecting video:

- Consider using a whiteboard or a piece of paper to write the prospect's name on. Alternatively, download the mobile app "Big" which allows you to do this digitally on your phone. This helps your video thumbnail reenforce that this video has been recorded just for them.
- Your message in your video should be similar to what you would have written in a prospecting email. It needs to be relevant and personalised, and to lead with problems.
- Keep it short and to the point (no more than 90 seconds).
- Practice before sending the video, but don't sound robotic. You want to deliver the message succinctly, but also to take advantage of the fact that people like videos as they feel more "human" than a written email, so they don't need to sound perfect.

- Make eye contact with the camera and smile!

Before sending your message, I've found referencing the video in the subject line works really well. I also entice the prospect into playing the video by putting an initial opening line/trigger event to explain why I have recorded the video. See the example below:

Also notice in the example above that you want to keep the amount of text to a minimum. The prospect must be able to see the entire email without having to scroll.

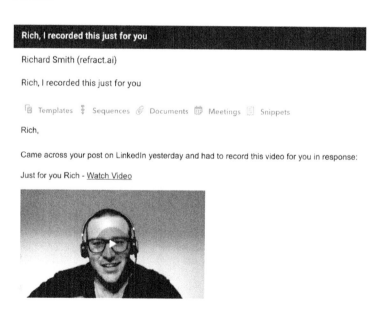

**Rich, I recorded this just for you**

Richard Smith (refract.ai)

Rich, I recorded this just for you

📋 Templates ↕ Sequences 📎 Documents 📅 Meetings 📄 Snippets

Rich,

Came across your post on LinkedIn yesterday and had to record this video for you in response:

Just for you Rich - Watch Video

Make sense to connect?

# Chapter Twelve

# Text Messaging as a 21st Century Prospecting Tool

Can you use text messaging as part of your prospecting workflow? Yes... but not all the time.

In this chapter we'll share with you how to use it.

I first started dabbling with text messaging after reading Tony J. Hughes' book *Combo Prospecting*. The book uses a boxing analogy, and suggests prospecting should be a "jab, jab, PUNCH" approach. All within a few minutes. An example would be:

- Cold call and if no answer, leave a voicemail or email and then...
- Send a text message informing them you tried to call/email and then....
- Connect on LinkedIn and say in the connection invite that you'd called/emailed and text.

The idea being, with so many jabs in quick succession that they can't ignore you.

I tried this approach for a few weeks, and had some success. But very little of that was a result of the text message element.

My conclusion was that, while everyone is different, texting before you've spoken to your prospect is too much, too soon. There is some irony here though. A high proportion of emails are read on a phone screen so why is texting different?

In my opinion, it feels different, as it's their phone number. It therefore feels more personal and perhaps intrusive when coming from a "stranger". It's possible this will change with future generations who embrace quick text messaging platforms like WhatsApp etc.

My advice is this: if they don't know you or you've not spoken before, then don't text. The exception of course is if they text you first –when cold calling mobile to mobile this isn't uncommon. Many times I've had a text message land after I've tried calling, saying something like:

*"Sorry, can't talk right now."*

If they text you first then it's fair game, and make sure you text back straight away.

So when can you text?

I believe once you've had an initial conversation you can text prospects, and the result is super effective. In fact, a whopping 98% of texts are opened and 90% of that is within the first three minutes!

The benefits of texting are twofold. Firstly, you're not competing with a busy inbox so the chances of them seeing and reading your message is about as high as you can get. Secondly, responses are quick and easy for a prospect, so it's ideal if you need a speedy response.

Here's some examples of where texting my prospects has worked really well for me.

**Responding to them:** As mentioned above, if they text you first, text back.

**Confirmation:** An example would be that you've just got off the phone, sent a calendar invite, and their email has bounced back. Send a quick text explaining what's happened and asking them to confirm their email.

**Checking availability:** You know when you get that prospect who's like trying to nail down smoke when it comes to a time and date for the next call? Send a text.

*"Hey, it's Mark @ Refract, when are you free to speak?"* – Often they end up just calling you back which is great, and at the very least you tend to get a reply about their availability.

**Reminders:** My local garage, dentist and doctors surgery are really good at this – sending a text the day before/ morning of my appointment. I always read them and it always reminds me. You can use text in the same way – as a quick reminder of an upcoming call.

**They fail to show up:** Let's imagine you have a call in the calendar for 3pm and they don't answer. Send a quick text such as:

*"I just tried to call, assuming now no longer works for you?"*

They're more likely to respond to this than an email in my experience, as it feels more personal. They feel like they've personally let you down, and it is easier to respond with a "sorry" and a new time that works.

**Reactivate:** Getting the cold shoulder? Have they started ignoring your calls and emails? Try a text. For the same reasons as mentioned above, this route might be your best chance of a response.

**When you need an instant answer:** For example, you're running late for your meeting and you need the best possible chance of ensuring they see your message in time.

Here's some real examples of text messages I've sent. In the example below I cold called a gentleman called Ian, mobile-to-mobile and he texted me back "can I call you later", so I texted back straight away and booked a meeting:

> Can I call you later?

> > Hey Ian, yeah, please do - we've not spoken before, my name is Mark. Keen to speak with you and share a couple of ideas that might not be on your radar with regards to how you currently coach sales teams in a sustainable and repeatable way. When works for you?

> Next week but I'm working today with clients using zoom

> ███@████████.co.uk

> Send an email and let's fix a time next week

> > Thanks Ian, I was wondering how 11am worked for you - either Tuesday, Wednesday or Friday?

> Would need to be Wednesday at 11am only one of those times I am free Send an invite. You using Zoom/Skype?

> > Yeah, Zoom. Great I'll send an invite shortly. Mark

> > Invite sent. Speak then. Thanks, Mark.

In this next example, I was waiting for my prospect to send me a calendar invite with her colleagues attached. I tried to call and had no luck. Her email was bouncing back so I dropped a quick text and she quickly called me back and sent the invite.

Hey Helen, it's Mark from Refract.

Just tried to call, wanted to give the gentlest of nudges to send me that calendar invite and your address

Mark

- PS, I did try to email you on; @ .com and it's bouncing back?

In the example below I was due to speak with Shane at 11am, but my train was delayed which meant that, if we were to speak, I'd be on a train with an unreliable signal. I needed to be confident Shane would see my message, so I texted him asking to rearrange:

> Hi Shane, I can still call at 11, I am, however unexpectedly caught on a train... would you have some time this afternoon? Anytime from 1-3:30? Or 4:30/5?

> Try me when you off the train. Or at 1

> 1pm would be perfect. Thank you Shane.

In the next example, I wanted to catch my prospect first thing in the morning. It was their first day back from a two-week holiday and we had a call scheduled for 9.30am. It was an important call and I wanted to make sure it went ahead.

I believe that, if I hadn't sent James the text, the chances of him missing our call would have been sky high. A quick text made sure I was at the top of his mind and the call went ahead.

> Morning James, appreciate its your first day back, hope you had a good break. Are we still good to catch up at 9:30 for 5 minutes to get our ducks in a row and set up for September 1st launch?

Morning Mark. All good here, hope you're well. Good for 9:30am, let's get agreed on the plan!

> Great, I'll fire up the zoom just before and email you the link 👍

In this final example, it was a bit of an emergency. I was meant to call a prospect in the car on my way home but my battery died. As soon as I got home, I dropped them a text to explain (I felt it was too late in the evening to call). I chose text as I felt I'd personally let Ben down and I therefore wanted to do it over text rather than with an email which would have felt more formal.

> Hey Ben, I've just got home - my battery died earlier today, hence me not calling at 5. Please accept my apologies. Are you free tomorrow? Either first thing or 4pm onwards?

> Evening Mark. No problem, it worked out quite well as I was dealing with a product crisis this end! Have you time Friday to catch up? I have a busy day tomorrow and marketing still haven't come back to me so gives them more time!

> Sure... anytime from 11am (except 1:30-3) - when's good with you?

> Okay. I should be off a train to Newcastle around 11:40 so that could work well. I don't suppose you'll be at UKONs?!

## Tips

Use text like you would normally, and by that I mean keep it short and conversational. If you want to be more formal then use the appropriate channel, such as email.

If you're not sure they'd welcome a text, then mention it on a call with them and gauge how they respond.

Finally, use it sparingly. I wouldn't use text as my main go-to channel with any one prospect. Use it as and when you need to in order to give you the best chance of a reply or if you're drinking in the last chance saloon.

# Chapter Thirteen

# How to Reduce the Dreaded 'No-Show'

There really is nothing worse than the dreaded no-show. OK, maybe there are some worse things... but it's still a pain in the arse.

Whether you're an SDR who's compensation is based on the number of qualified meetings that take place, or an AE who's spent 10 minutes preparing in advance of the call, it's equally frustrating.

The truth is, there are many reasons why prospects don't show up. We'll never make every prospect turn up, because life happens. Their boss needs that last minute report; a family emergency; hell – they might have just forgotten about you.

That said, as an ambitious salesperson we need to look at ourselves and take charge of the things which are in our control. We need to formulate a plan that makes even the flakiest of prospects desperate to speak with us.

The main reason prospects don't show up is because, as a salesperson, we didn't do a good enough job of getting them excited. We've all had examples where we have booked that meeting in with more hope than expectation that the prospect will show up. And that's a waste of everyone's time.

However, if you read this book and put the hints and tips into action then this shouldn't be an issue for you much longer. You'll soon be getting your prospects so excited they are looking forward to speaking with you again.

So, once we've booked that awesome meeting with your ICP let's talk about what you can do next to make sure you get to speak with them again.

### Booking the next step ASAP

The first mistake eager reps make is asking the prospect when they are free. It sounds a bit like this:

*"Great stuff Mrs Prospect. When would be a good time to speak again?"*

How does the prospect respond? They look at their calendar and because they're "oh so busy", they suggest a time at least a week in advance. We all know time kills deals so we need to take control. Try something like this instead:

*"Great stuff Mrs. Prospect, do you have any time at all for a call this afternoon, or failing that tomorrow?"*

We all know people like to take an option if we give them one. Most will opt for tomorrow. ***Spoiler alert*** Their calendars are never as busy as they make out.

If they disagree and try to push you a week or more into the future, don't be scared to challenge them. I say something like this.

*"Maybe I've misread the situation Mrs. Prospect. It sounded like you were as excited as me about continuing our conversation and finding out how we can help you solve X. Would it be fair to say if you aren't available for the next two weeks, this isn't a priority for you right now?"*

If you've done a good job, most will push back and tell you they are keen to speak with you, and they'll expand upon the reason they gave you the time/date they originally suggested.

If they agree it isn't a priority, then you might as well qualify them out as early as possible. Remember, we need to spend our time with prospects who want our help.

If there's a genuine reason why the meeting has to take place a week or more in the future, then we need to keep our prospects engaged.

An easy way to do this is to share relevant content between meetings. A simple email with a blog link will do. The aim here isn't to try and sell your product or service, it's to stop your prospects forgetting about you.

Like I said, some prospects genuinely forget. I know – how dare they forget you after such a memorable email or cold call. Prospects will forget you, so don't take it personally.

We can do a number of things to make sure our prospects don't forget about us.

The easiest thing to do that most forget about, is to schedule reminder emails. Tools like Calendly will allow you to schedule these in advance so you don't have to remember to send them yourself.

We send a reminder email the morning of the meeting, an hour in advance, and then five minutes before. Include the conference call details in the last email you send, so it's as easy as possible for your prospect to join you, and they don't have to dig out the call details.

Another tip is to connect with your prospect on LinkedIn. Don't forget to send them a personalised message as part of your connection request telling them you're looking forward to meeting with them. All of these little tactics humanise you and keep you familiar. The more familiar you are to your prospect the less likely they are to no-show.

**Sending effective calendar invites**

Sending poor, lazy calendar invites is a common mistake a lot of sales reps make.

Here's an example of a typical calendar invite I receive:

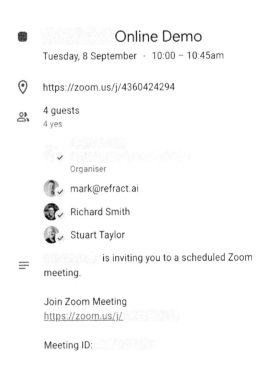

Seriously, what on earth is that?

Think about it. The rep in this example has done all the hard work to get to the point where I've agreed to a meeting.

They've carried out research, tried multiple times and channels to reach me, and convinced me it's worth setting up a demo. Why then, go and spoil it by sending a half-arsed invite with little to no detail? It is just laziness and there's no excuse for it.

Your calendar invites should promote the next call, explain the purpose (the problems they have and how you're going to eradicate them) and include an agenda.

Why? I want you to put yourself in the shoes of your prospect for a second. Imagine you've answered a cold call and you've agreed to the next step, which is a discovery call.

Seven days later, it's the day of that discovery call with the sales rep you spoke to.

As always, you have a busy day ahead and then something unexpected comes up. Perhaps a colleague asks if you're free at the time of the discovery call for an internal meeting (again, easy to imagine!).

You check your calendar and all you see is a half-arsed invite that has some screen-share details. You have two choices:

A: Think back to the cold call and remind yourself what the discovery call is about or dig out an email and then tell yourself why you need to be on this call. You then tell your colleague you're busy at that time.

OR

B: You can just hit the decline button, no show, and take the meeting your colleague has asked you to attend.

The vast majority will choose option B. It's easy, and it requires no thought. A poor calendar invite is giving your prospect a job. You're asking them to remember why they said yes and the purpose of the call. It's not happening. It's too easy to cancel.

A good calendar invite helps your prospect. It's like a little recap at the start of your favourite TV show, as it reminds them of their reasons for wanting to speak again.

A good calendar invite is easy to write, and often reusable from prospect to prospect. And trust me, it significantly reduces no shows. Don't waste the efforts you've made to get to this point. Give yourself the best chance of getting your prospect to turn up for the call.

Here are some examples of some calendar invites I've sent out. All of my prospects in these examples turned up for the next call. How could they not?

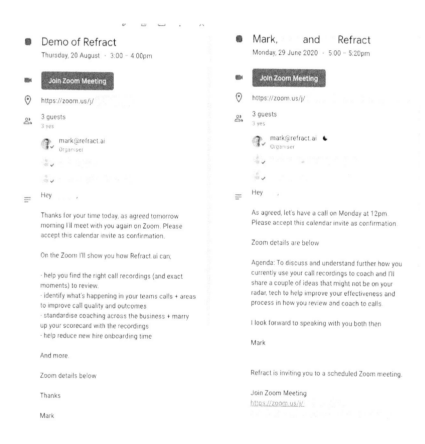

Notice all invites include the line:

*'Please accept this calendar invite as confirmation.'*

That's a carefully chosen sentence. In my experience, those that accept an invite are far more likely to turn up than those who don't as they feel more committed.

If someone doesn't accept the invite you must email them the day before and say "I notice you've not accepted the invite, are we still on?"

Never send a lazy calendar invite again! There's no excuses.

**\*Top Tip:** The day before your scheduled call, you should be confirming with your prospect by sending them a quick email to confirm they're still available for the call. When the prospect replies confirming they're still good to speak, edit the invite and add "[confirmed]" to the start of the subject line. This does two things. Firstly, it triggers an update in their calendar notifying them of the "[confirmed]" status, reinforcing the meeting. Secondly, it makes it harder for them to 'no show' as they know they've double confirmed with you.

# [Confirmed] Call: Jenny & Mark

27 Oct 2020    1:00pm  to  2:00pm    27 Oct 2020    Time zone

☐ All day   Doesn't repeat ▾

**SDR to AE handoffs**

If you're responsible for booking meetings for another member of the team then there's a few extra things you need to do.

Firstly, you need to make the prospect aware of exactly what is going to happen.

If your AE will be running the next stage of the sales process, you need to inform the prospect so it doesn't come as a surprise.

This is also an opportunity to sell your colleague to your prospect. Remember to also give a reason as to why your colleague will be taking things from here.

Here's the script we use:

*"What I'm going to do Mrs. Prospect is try and see if I can schedule a call with my colleague Mark. He's our resident expert and specialises in working with companies like yours so I'd like to secure him for the conversation if he's available, let me check...."*

*\*Pause for five seconds while you check calendars.\**

*"Great. Mark is free this afternoon at 3pm or tomorrow morning at 10am. Which works best for you?"*

Bigging up your colleague is a great way to position them as an expert. This makes the prospect feel special that you've gone out of your way to get the best guy or girl for them. It's also easier for your colleague to become a trusted advisor when they speak to your prospect.

Once this is done, the AE needs to take over and send an introductory email.

It doesn't need to be *War And Peace*: a line or two will suffice. It needs to let the prospect know they've spoken to the SDR about the opportunity, they're excited about continuing the conversation, and

> **8:30am Tomorrow**
>
> Hey Gerard,
>
> My colleague Nia has secured 8:30am tomorrow in our calendars for an introductory call.
>
> Ahead of then, I wanted to quickly introduce myself and share my contact details. I'm Mark, and I head up the New Business team.
>
> The purpose of this call is to share a couple of fresh ideas with you that may or may not be on your radar. My focus will be on sharing how conversation intelligence and call coaching technology could help your team review more customer facing conversations in less time as well as improve the quality and outcome of those calls.
>
> I'll call you on XXXXXXXXXXX
>
> Thanks
>
> Mark

they're going to do some research in advance. See an example below:

Mentioning research in advance is a good idea as it makes the prospect feel you're putting time and effort into speaking with them. This makes them more likely to turn up to the meeting and feel almost like they'll be letting you down if they don't turn up.

The next and final point is an important one. Don't be late and do everything in your power not to reschedule.

**What if they no-show? Send a reactivation email.**

From time to time you'll get a no show. It's inevitable. I'd always suggest picking up the phone to rebook in the first instance. However, if you can't reach them on the phone, the next best thing is sending a reactivation email.

A reactivation email is a stripped back email, just a short, direct message asking your prospect if they're still interested in speaking with you. By stripped back, I mean no fancy email signature, no previous chain: just one sentence and straight to the point.

Here's an example of a good reactivation email:

, quick question...

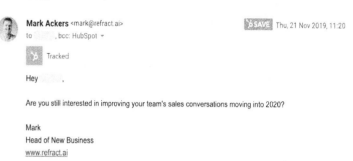

**Mark Ackers** <mark@refract.ai>            SAVE   Thu, 21 Nov 2019, 11:20
to          , bcc: HubSpot ▾

   Tracked

Hey          ,

Are you still interested in improving your team's sales conversations moving into 2020?

Mark
Head of New Business
www.refract.ai

Notice the subject line. This plays on the curiosity of the prospect and entices them to open it. I've done the research and this subject line has seen me get an 86% open rate.

The body of the email is simply:

> Hey [first name},
>
> Are you still interested in [enter key problem you solve] moving into 2020?
>
> Mark

Naturally, you can play around with this sentence but the key is to ask one direct question, focused on whether they are still interested in solving the problem you've spoken to them about before.

That's it.

I've played around with the question and seen response rates sit at the 38% mark, however the email above generated a 57% open rate.

Below is the response that I received back to this email:

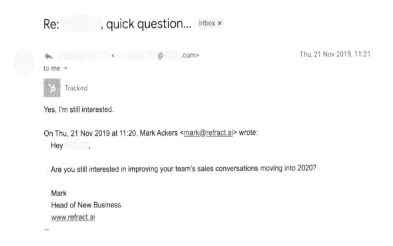

Notice the time of the response? it's sixty seconds later.

229

I picked up the phone and, within five weeks, they were a paying customer.

I genuinely believe that among all of the tips and tricks in this book, the reactivation email is one of the best plays we're sharing. You will have so many prospects you can send a reactivation email to: just look back at anyone who didn't buy in the past and/or anyone who failed to turn up for a meeting. Start sending reactivation emails out today. It's low-hanging fruit.

# Chapter Fourteen

# Build Your Own Brand and Be Seen as an Expert

Many salespeople will hear the phrase "build your brand" and quietly cringe inside. The reality is that due to the sheer volume and noise our prospects are dealing with, they have become more selective about who they pay attention to. In this chapter we'll help you build an authentic online brand to help you sell yourself to prospects and be seen as a true expert as opposed to the average salesperson.

Learn from your customers

In order to be seen as an expert, you have to truly understand your customer.

Most salespeople think they understand their customer, simply because they've gone through some induction training at their company or have been to a series of sales meetings with their prospects. But here's the stark reality. If you haven't walked in the shoes of your customer, how can you possibly claim to understand their pleasures, frustrations, desires, challenges, and the things which grind their gears?

For example, how many salespeople who sell construction project management software have ever worked on a construction site?

How many salespeople who sell technology for restaurant owners have ever run a restaurant?

I'd say very few… if any at all.

The problem with just assuming you understand your prospect is that when you start to pitch them or engage in conversations, the way you communicate the problems you think your product or service solves is often articulated in the way your Marketing Team has told you to articulate it. The message just doesn't hit the right notes with your prospect and you've lost them before the conversation even got started.

I remember once speaking with a salesperson who sold vehicle-leasing services to small, local, businesses. I asked him what problems his customers faced which they helped solve, and this was his response:

*"Customers would benefit from having a leased vehicle rather than owning one as it means they don't pay maintenance costs and they can upgrade every year."*

However, when I asked the owner of a local plumbing company, who had leased three vans with the salesperson's company, this is what he told me:

*"I had a nightmare situation last year when my van broke down and had to be in the garage for 48 hours. We had to cancel two jobs at short notice and it hit me in the pocket"*

Can you see the difference? The salesperson's interpretation of the problems he solves sounds and feels very different from what his prospects say.

When you start to speak the language of your prospects, your whole messaging resonates more. Not only does this help with prospecting, it also impacts your ability to be seen as an expert and someone who is genuinely helpful.

## Interview your customers

One of the quickest ways you can better understand your prospects...is to speak with your customers. Crazy, right?

But how many salespeople have proactively contacted an existing customer, and asked for 10 to 15 minutes of their time to talk through their specific reasons as to why they bought?

Written case studies may help somewhat here. But I've always found that case studies have had too much "polish" put on them by Marketing, and thus won't present a true reflection of your customer's words.

You may even want to buy the customer a gift e-voucher for a free Starbucks or similar as a thank you for their time. It would be a small price to pay for an invaluable activity, and I think you'd be surprised at how many are willing to help.

My recommendation here is to record these interviews on Zoom. This allows you to focus on the conversation and play it back afterwards, so you're not relying on memory. In addition, these videos become incredible mini-testimonials which you can use (with permission) as powerful content to share on LinkedIn or to send to prospects after initial conversations with them. BOOM!

Here's an email example below, which you can steal to create interviews with your customers:

---

Hi Jason,

As a valued customer of Refract, wondering if you can help me out.

I'm hoping to get better informed about why customers specifically bought from us -so I can do a better job when speaking with others who may benefit from working with us. Would you be open to an informal chat with me to share your own experiences?

This should only take 15 minutes, would be recorded on Zoom (so I can play back and take notes). In return, I'll send you a £5 voucher for a Starbucks on me.

---

Note that I don't use the word "interview". Interviews sound too formal and too much of a big commitment. Informal chats sound exactly like what they are!

One of the most interesting parts of this exercise is that you typically end up finding out the additional reasons your customers love your product now they have been using it for some time. These are often some of the most enlightening factors in helping you better understand your customers as it goes beyond "why they bought" to "how is it helping them succeed right now?".

Here are some of the questions you can use as part of these customer interviews:

1.    Talk me through the problem you were looking to solve by buying our product?
2.    Can you share with me a couple of real-life stories of you running into these problems?
3.    How did these problems make you feel at the time?
4.    Did these problems cost you time? Money? Stress? Frustration?
5.    How did you initially see how our product could specifically help you do things better?
6.    How do you describe our product to people you talk to?

7.     After using our product for some time, did you experience any additional benefits beyond the initial reasons you bought?

## Listen to sales call recordings

One of the many benefits of listening to sales call recordings is that you get to hear for yourself the challenges mentioned by prospects before they buy.

I remember once listening to a call recording of Mark's, and learned the following tactic. He was on a late-stage call with a prospect and asked the following question:

*"If you decided to move forward with us, what would be the reasons?"*

In response, the prospect explained, in their own words, the specific reasons as to why they were buying. What was most revealing was that the key reasons the prospect gave were actually different to Mark's expectations. In addition, the prospect ended up explaining all of the personal motivations they had for buying. It was a classic case of getting the prospect selling the product themselves, while also allowing the salesperson to get a better understanding of the customer's point of view.

## Interview your prospects

I once read an article explaining how sick and tired the author was of always being emailed by salespeople, and always being asked for their time. She was fed up of having their inboxes filled every day with emails from salespeople pitching her and asking her for "30 minutes" or if she "wanted a demo".

Once again this made me think. What if I emailed prospects not with the intention of pitching them my product, but simply to ask for their expertise? Human nature dictates that people like the idea of being seen as an expert or, at the very least, to be given a platform for their opinion on something they are passionate about.

So I carried out the following process, which at the first attempt landed me 20 conversations with my ideal prospects from one email (after sending it to 50 people in total). I've replicated this process a number of times since and had similar results.

Step 1: Build a list of your ideal prospects. Make sure these are carefully selected and people whom you wish to build a relationship with.

Step 2: Create an email template which is personalised to the extent that it references things which your prospect would be interested in, and has relevance to their job role.

Step 3: Make the objective of the email to get their thoughts and opinions on a specific, current industry topic. The key here is ensuring it is connected to a problem which your product or service solves.

Step 4: Ensure that it's clear the prospect gets something in return. (In other words, answer the question: "What's in it for me?" which we can abbreviate as WIIFM.) In the example below, the WIIFM is that I will plug the prospect and their company in an article which I'll publish.

Step 5: Do NOT come across sales-y. Prospects will sniff this out a mile away. Treat it purely as an exercise to learn more about your prospects... not to pitch them.

Step 6: Send to all.

Here's an example email I recently sent using this process, about the impact COVID 19 has had on sales teams going remote. I sent this to 20 Chief Revenue Officers and had 8 positive responses:

Bas

I came across your name recently, after researching some of the most influential CRO's in fast-growth tech companies in the UK, and was hoping you could contribute to an article I'm writing.

Not sure if you saw this article in Forbes? It provided advice on leading remote sales teams in a crisis, and shared the staggering statistic that less than 6% of companies were properly equipped for working from home at the start of the year.

Another article I read from last year, claimed that actually - remote working is becoming the norm and is only going to increase.

I plan to write a blog post on the topic, and would love to get your perspective Bas, on the challenges and opportunities associated with leading remote tech sales teams. Perhaps I can get a quote from you?

If you're open to having this chat over the phone, heres a link to my calendar so you can book in 15 minutes

Rich

P.S I have a reasonably engaged and growing audience on LinkedIn. I'll be sure to give you and your company a plug in return.

I conducted the recorded interviews on Zoom and each took about 20 minutes. What was enlightening about the interviews is how open prospects were, often willingly giving insight into their challenges without me really trying too hard to find out. Maybe this was because they knew this wasn't a sales conversation, so didn't have their guard up in the usual way?

And guess what happens on almost every interview? The prospect finishes by saying: "Tell me about what you do".

Not only do the interviews give me a pipeline of warm prospects for me to engage with down the line, but they also make me more informed about the challenges facing my prospects, in their own words. Furthermore, it gives me the content to write impactful industry articles, which I then post and share on LinkedIn. This reaps the reward of generating engagement and connections with similar prospects who read the article. It also achieves my key goal of being seen as an expert and trusted advisor.

Take this process and template above, customise it for your own audience and start getting to know your prospects better today!

## Using LinkedIn to build your brand

When I started in sales, social media was at its early adopter stage. Facebook was starting to boom among the younger audience; people were trying to figure out what on earth Twitter was all about; Instagram didn't exist; and LinkedIn was nothing more than an online CV site.

Fast forward to 2020, and social media – in particular LinkedIn – has become a crucial instrument in the salesperson's toolbox. (Check out Chapter Ten for more help here)

LinkedIn is now the biggest opportunity salespeople have to expand their network and generate a huge pipeline, outside of more traditional methods such as phone or email. Not only this, but the huge global reach of this great platform, when utilised to its full potential, has the ability to catapult you into being seen as a true expert in your industry, and to open up massive opportunities beyond just filling your funnel.

However, the problem is that the significant majority of salespeople whose target audience exist and "hang out" on LinkedIn still see it as nothing more than a place to update their "digital CV" when job hunting, or to generically pitch prospects (with poor results). There is a huge opportunity being missed by the masses. Be honest with yourself: is this you?

Salespeople need to recognise the importance of building their brand in order to stand out from the noise. It may sound a little bit cringey, but hear me out. It's no coincidence that when I'm hiring for salespeople, I always go straight to their LinkedIn profile before looking at their CV. I want to see how much they are leveraging LinkedIn as a means to build their brand and audience. I want answers to questions like whether they are demonstrating their expertise through the content they post, and how much effort they have put into building a solid network to help them sell. From conversations with many other sales leaders, it is clear they also do this.

Sadly, too many salespeople have built little to no brand. And it's hurting them. Ironically those who just use LinkedIn as a digital CV are ultimately letting themselves down when it comes to selling themselves.

About two years ago, I decided to go "all-in" on LinkedIn. This has led to the following:

- Hundreds of meetings being generated for me and my sales team with ideal prospects, with no "cold-prospecting" involved.
- Being invited to speak on stage at industry events.
- Being invited to appear as a guest on a number of leading sales podcasts.
- "Side-Gig" coaching engagements.
- Huge website traffic for my company.
- Job offers.
- Getting listed in various "Top 50/Top 100" sales publications.
- Forming valuable connections with influential people in the sales world who will become advocates of myself and my company.

This may sound like I'm bragging, and the truth is, I often feel a bit embarrassed when I get invited on to podcasts. The reality is that I have far less experience in sales than many and relative to my public profile I've possibly achieved far less than others. But at the same time, I recognised the power of utilising LinkedIn as a content site rather than just a networking platform. Combine this with my experience, commitment, and opinions, and I've been able to leverage it as rocket fuel in my career success.

## Writing content on LinkedIn

Following on from the huge success of their "Pulse" publishing platform, which enabled users to publish articles in blog format, the trend quickly switched to writing content more informally in "long/short post format". This took the Facebook model of writing long-form "statuses", and enabled users to make their content more visual and more accessible to their connections.

Here are some golden rules for a successful LinkedIn content strategy:

- **Consistency is king** : Like anything in life, great results need commitment and consistency. Just as working out once a week won't help you lose weight, writing content sporadically will mean you struggle to get serious traction. About 18 months ago I made the decision to post content once a day Monday-Friday, and I have largely succeeded in doing so. Many people write just a couple of posts, don't get the desired results and give up. Write good stuff consistently, and you'll eventually build an audience. It's a marathon, not a sprint.

- **Stories sell:** The best content I post comes from my own real experiences in sales. This means the calls, demos, and work experiences I have day-to-day. Because I sell to sales leaders, it's likely that the stories I share will often resonate with them. The key thing here is telling stories which speak to your audience. As you are in sales, you live and breathe experiences connected to your market and industry every day. You should therefore never be short of some insight, opinions, and stories which will connect with your audience when you share them.

- **Don't be afraid to polarise opinion:** The nature of the LinkedIn algorithm dictates that the more engagement on a post (likes/comments etc), the more traction and visibility it will get on feeds. The thing which garners comments is often a topic which generates a variety of opinions. Don't be afraid to speak with your true voice and be authentic;

accept that not everybody will agree with you (and that's not a bad thing). But at the same time, be conscious that LinkedIn is a professional platform so you mustn't overstep the mark. A badly worded post, or one that is deemed to be offensive can cause more harm than good.

- **Don't post to pitch your product/service:** The type of content which is sure to turn your prospects off is anything which is obviously a product pitch. Any time I've veered into this swim lane, it's not given me good results. People want to engage with content which they perceive to be valuable or useful. A post which is all about your product or service will just be perceived as being "all about you". Think of the content you post as something which will start conversations with your prospects. At the very least, it will increase the visibility of you and your company. This is why having a fully optimised LinkedIn profile is so crucial.

- Practice your writing as much as your sales skills: Writing great copy is a skill in itself. Great copywriting is as crucial to your content's success as the content itself. Badly worded content which doesn't flow or have good structure can often lose its impact. I've found that the quality of my writing has improved over time (and can still get better). Look at the posts which get great traction on LinkedIn from others, and try and learn from them.

- **Be authentic**: It seems obvious, but it's important that the content you post comes from the heart, is authentic, and intentional. Part of building a brand is people buying into you as a person. Nobody wants to follow a robot or someone they don't really believe is being themselves.

**Other useful considerations:**

- Try and ensure that you post a blend of content. Not everything should be a text post (although for some reason these always seem to perform better). Mix it up with video, images, and sharing other people's content, with your own perspectives attached to it. Your followers can get tired of seeing the same content formats.

- For video/audio posts, ensure you add subtitles onto the media file. This is because a lot of your followers will be accessing LinkedIn and viewing the content with their audio on silent (while they are on the move, commuting, or in public spaces). There are lots of websites which will allow you to add subtitles on your content for free, and others will do this for you automatically for a reasonably small fee. Subtitles can also make your video appear more professional.

- LinkedIn does not like its users to link to external websites. As such, the algorithm punishes posts which include hyperlinks to third-parties and restricts the visibility of the post on feeds. If you are going to post a link, make sure you post the link in the "comments" area of your post and reference where the link can be found in the body of your post.

- Building a strong follower base can be achieved rapidly by posting thoughtful and meaningful comments on other people's posts. It shouldn't all be about your own content. I've sometimes got more engagement on a comment I've added to somebody else's post than I have on my own! Make sure you spend time interacting with other people's content as this also encourages them to reciprocate.

- Try and respond to comments on your posts with comments back. This not only shows a polite acknowledgement of people who take the time to interact with you, but also bear in mind that the more comments there are, the more opinions and the more visibility your post will have.

- Invest time every day making connections with your target types of people. These are the people you want to see your content. The people who you connect with are often some of those most likely to see the next content you post.

## How to create killer LinkedIn posts:

To finish off this chapter, I thought I would provide a breakdown of how to create killer LinkedIn posts which get traction and help you start conversations with your prospects.

First of all, as with any prospecting technique, start with something which gets people intrigued and wanting to find out more. A useful way of doing this, is to start by asking a thought-provoking question. Strengthen this by basing the question on something which is likely to come across as opinionated. The key here is to get the prospect hungry to read on:

 **Richard Smith**
Frustrated your team's sales calls don't close? Crave a team of top perfor...
6mo · Edited · ⊕

Why do sales people get so obsessed with needing to have expert 'product knowledge'?

Next, bring some context as to why you've asked the question. A useful way of doing this is to share a personal story. Remember from the guidelines provided above that stories sell and often resonate best with your audience. In this real-life example post, my opinion is based on my experiences of interviewing salespeople:

I've lost count of how many people I've interviewed, and one of the main things they tell me they want to become expert in within their first month is 'the product'.

It's why so many become expert 'product pitchers' versus expert sales people.

Following on from this, you want to build your argument and point of view. What I aim to do here is to express opinions which really sing to the problems my prospects are facing. In my case, because I am selling to sales leaders I want to address the frustrations they are battling with. These are around their salespeople being ineffective in their sales conversations, product pitching too much, and ultimately not closing enough deals or booking enough meetings.

---

Heres the thing...

Being an expert in the product is not the thing which is going to help you sell more.

Sure, you need to have a good understanding of your product's capabilities. You need to be able to hold your own when answering questions. But theres things you can become more accomplished in, which will increase the chances of customers buying from you:

---

Next, I'll aim to express my expertise on this topic. By this point of the post, I want my audience to be thinking "Yep...that's a problem which resonates, but what's the solution?" I've found listing the "better alternative way of doing things", provides the audience with valuable, practical guidance. I also want them to see me as somebody who could be the medicine for the problem they have, so they will come to my profile, engage with me directly, or simply just start following me on LinkedIn.

---

- Asking great lines of questions to help prospects see a problem they didn't realise they had

- Asking questions which get prospects sharing more about their struggles

- Sharing powerful stories of how similar customers succeeded by working with you.

- Sharing insights with your prospects which position you as an expert in your field

- Actively listening to what prospects tell you, so you can pick up on emotive nuggets

---

Finally, I'll sign off on the post with a short and sweet summary opinion, or maybe pose a question to the audience to encourage their engagement. Note that this post generated a reasonably high number of comments (not just likes). Many of those comments were not just people agreeing with me either...this was key to the post getting traction and close to 40,000 views:

The best sales people barely talk about their products/services. Stop obsessing over it.

#makesalesconversationsgreatagain

 410 · 87 Comments

Reactions

👍 Like   💬 Comment   ➡ Share                     Most Relevant ▼

📈 38,674 views of your post in the feed

# Chapter Fifteen

# LinkedIn Tips and Tricks

The following are additional "tips and tricks" we've picked up over the years when using LinkedIn to prospect. Note that, for some of them, a subscription to LinkedIn Sales Navigator is required.

**Sending Connection Requests**

There is a lot of debate about the "do's and don'ts" when connecting with prospects on LinkedIn. The biggest thing to avoid is sending generic messages as part of your connection request, like "Hope we can connect", as this will come across as spammy. I've actually found that there is far more to be gained by not putting ANY message whatsoever in your connection requests than spending copious amounts of time personalising. This allows you to build your connection base quickly, and prospects tend to still accept as long as you look like a relevant connection for them. That is why your "headline" in your profile is so important (find out more about this in Chapter Ten). Building your connection base with relevant prospects, influencers, and thought leaders is crucial to maximising your content reach.

Please note that LinkedIn currently has a cap of 30,000 connections for individuals, so you may want to consider being selective about who you connect with.

### Accepting Connection Requests

It can be particularly exciting when someone who looks to be an ideal prospect sends you a connection request. However, when this happens, the worst thing you can do is respond to the prospect with a sales pitch. This is a surefire way of getting the prospect to regret connecting with you, and to not respond.

So, what should you do? I've found a winning formula here is to ask the prospect a question they will find hard to not respond to. Here it comes…

*"Thanks for connecting with me. Have we spoken before?"*

This question entices the prospect to respond, as they are quick to reassure that we don't in fact know each other, and also to explain the reason why they decided to connect with me. It's a key conversation starter, and even better, it can sometimes unveil a specific challenge or pain point the prospect is looking to you to help solve. Being provocative is key to prospecting success. Below is a real example of me deploying this tactic with someone who sent me a connection request. In fact, three months later, this same prospect became a customer!

 **Richard Smith** · 10:41 PM
Thanks for the connection

Have we spoken before?

Rich

· 10:47 PM
We haven't Rich
Just growing my network and your background and business could be useful to us at some point in the future

## Using Sales Navigator Insights for Trigger Events

One of the key benefits of LinkedIn Sales Navigator are the filters available to support advanced lead searches. Some of these I find more valuable than others, and I've highlighted these below.

Note that, in the example, I have run a basic search of Sales Leaders in the UK and US to start with.

## 29K+
### Changed jobs in past 90 days

*Changed jobs in the past 90 days.* This filter will show you prospects who have recently started a new role. For many in sales, a new role is often a key trigger event (or reason for getting in touch), as prospects entering new roles will typically have big personal objectives they are working towards and will often be looking at products or services to help support that.

## 85
### Mentioned in the news in past 30 days

*Mentioned in the news in the past 30 days.* This filter really helps when looking for personalisation ideas before reaching out to prospects. It will show you recent articles where the prospect has been mentioned and often some useful snippets or quotations which you can leverage in your cold messages, emails, or calls.

**150K+**
**Posted on LinkedIn in past 30 days**

*Posted on LinkedIn in the past 30 days.* This is also useful for finding those prospects who are actively posing content on LinkedIn and for the specific posts they have made, which can be useful personalisation material.

**161**
**Leads that follow your company on LinkedIn**

*Leads that follow your company on LinkedIn.* This is HUGE, and so often missed by sales reps when using Sales Navigator. This filter will show you prospects who are following your company page on LinkedIn. This not only tells you that these prospects have some level of interest in your company, but they will also be more familiar with you when it comes to reaching out to them. This warms up the cold approach, and will increase your chances of having a productive dialogue.

**Using Sales Navigator Smart Links**

A recent update to the Sales Navigator toolkit is the ability to create "Smart Links" which you can send to prospects. In a nutshell, a Smart Link is a link to a specific resource, but one which will give you analytics as to which prospect has viewed the resource.Crucially, it will also show the length of time they were viewing it. Below is an example of where I have added a whitepaper behind a Smart Link, and a list of prospects who have viewed the content.

Note the length of time Kavish spent viewing the content versus Brian or Chelsea. This is a strong indication that Kavish is more engaged with the material, and therefore will likely be a better prospect for me to contact.

**Winning with Remote Sales in a Downturn**
Created on August 13 · Last viewed on Saturday

---

›   Mohammed Ziyed HADFI ♦ محمد زياد الهادفي  accessed for 32 seconds

›   Chelsea Parker  accessed for 1 second

›   Chelsea Parker

›   Chelsea Parker  accessed for 26 seconds

›   Brian McDowell  accessed for 2 seconds

›   Brian McDowell  accessed for 1 minute

›   Kavish Gakhar  accessed for 5 seconds

›   Kavish Gakhar  accessed for 25 minutes

## Creating Lead Lists to track movement of your prospects

One of the best ways to keep track of your very best prospects, is to create a "Lead List" on LinkedIn Sales Navigator. This is a consolidated and custom list view of leads. It is a really effective way to identify the

264

activity of a highly targeted selection of people you are interested in contacting or staying in touch with. This is particularly useful for those salespeople who have an account-based Marketing (ABM) approach, which is a strategy based on focusing resources on a highly selective number of targeted accounts. If this is you, then create a Lead List of desirable prospects in your target accounts. Use this list view to engage with content your target prospects are posting on a daily basis, as well as researching different people within the same company.

For me, the most useful application of Lead Lists is to track the activity and movement of individuals who I have signed up as clients and those prospects who have previously committed to meeting with me. Given that people frequently move companies, this allows me to be alerted by LinkedIn when someone has started a new role, and the familiarity I already have with that prospect will increase my chances of meeting with them again. A warm approach will always trump a cold one.

# Chapter Sixteen

# The Winning Prospector's Tech Stack

In this chapter I'll share with you the technology we utilise in our roles when prospecting.

**Sales Navigator**

There's over 645 million LinkedIn profiles. How do you find the ones you should be prospecting? Sales Navigator is the answer. It's a paid upgrade for your LinkedIn account designed specifically for sales reps to help them find, contact and speak with their ICPs.

This, in my opinion, is non-negotiable. Fortunately the vast majority of companies will buy their sales reps Sales Navigator. If your employer is unwilling to invest, then start looking for an alternative employer. In my career I've only heard of this a handful of times but I have no doubt that there will be readers who will fall into this category. Trust me, if they're unwilling to invest into this essential tool they're unlikely to ever invest in anything that will help you. Look elsewhere.

There are three types of upgrades for Sales Navigator: Individual, Team, and Enterprise. All have the same base features but the volume and cost increases.

The benefits of upgrading to Sales Navigator include:

- Send InMail messages per month (20, 30 or 50 depending on package).
- Saved leads (1,500, 5,000 or 10,000 depending on package).
- Advanced lead and company search.
- Build custom search lists.
- Lead and account alerts.
- Notes and tags.

Team and Enterprise includes a couple of additional features; Team Link, CRM integration and out-of-network unlocks.

The two biggest benefits of Sales Navigator are the ability to find and access more contacts and build prospecting lists. InMails are okay, but personally I will only send one if I have had no luck with the phone and email.

My top tip with Sales Nav is to make sure you know how to properly use the search functionality when list building. It looks easy enough and you'll likely feel comfortable building lists. It will be more effective however, if you spend a bit of time properly reading how to use the keyword search, how to use Boolean logic and so forth. Check out Chapter Two for more guidance.

**Grammarly**

When reaching out to a prospect, a poorly written email with obvious spelling mistakes, typos or bad grammar can immediately turn a prospect off. The built-in spell checker is pretty helpful but it's not to be relied on. We use Grammarly, as it's a free writing assistant that goes above and beyond the standard spellchecker.

Download the plug-in and it will check your emails and help with spelling, typos, and grammar. It will also analyse sentence structure and provide alternative words or phrases to help you articulate your point.

You can keep the website open, and copy and paste your emails or proposals into the website for additional comfort.

If spelling and grammar is a weakness of yours, it could seriously be holding you back from further success. Buyers will question your credibility if you send a poorly written email.

While it's a free tool, there is also a paid version of Grammarly with additional benefits for as little as £9/$11 a month. That's a modest investment if you feel you're likely to be making mistakes in your emails.

**Data Subscription Companies**

Building LinkedIn lists is extremely helpful but there's a missing piece – contact information. The good news is that there are a number of companies that can provide you with your prospect's data such as their work email address, direct dial and mobile phone numbers.

In the past we've used ZoomInfo, which has now been acquired by their competitor DiscoverOrg, the biggest player in the market. We currently use

LeadIQ. We switched because we felt the data for our ICP was better and the price was significantly less. Another company we've looked at is Cognism. There are many similar companies out there. My advice would be to speak with a couple of providers, as they will all provide you with sample data and free trials. This will help you work out who has the best data for you and your ICP.

I'll show how we use LeadIQ.

Once we find an ideal prospect, you can click on the LeadIQ plugin and a pop up presents itself next to the LinkedIn profile. You'll see in the example below that I can click to reveal their email and/or mobile phone number. I can also save this information straight into our CRM, HubSpot.

I have found this type of tool to be a game-changer and I'd encourage you to get your company to invest.

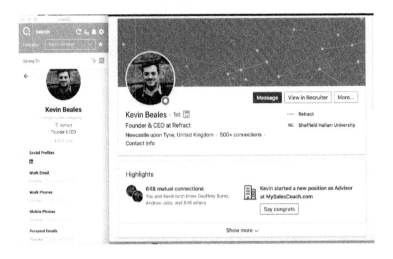

## Video Prospecting

Many sales reps will tell you video prospecting is the way forward – I'm not entirely sure myself, although I can say I have always watched a video when it's been made for me, although it doesn't happen often. Tools like Loom, Wistia, Vidyard are free chrome plugins that tap into your webcam and let you record yourself, meaning you can make a quick video for your prospect.

Typically, to show this video is custom made for the individual, the video starts with the rep holding a small whiteboard with the prospect's name written on it.

In my opinion, video prospecting works better with some personas and profiles of customers better than others. In SaaS it's a bit passé whereas if I was selling in, for example, the hospitality sector, I believe it would be unique and help you stand out.

My advice is to try it as you have absolutely nothing to lose and everything to gain. Check out chapter eleven for some more best practices here.

## Sales Engagement Platforms

Outreach & SalesLoft are two of the biggest platforms out there. HubSpot also has prospecting workflows/sequencing capabilities. These platforms go above and beyond, helping you prospect productively. Adopting these platforms is going to be a company decision due to pricing structure.

If you're self-funded and in need of a tool to help accelerate your prospecting then you should look at MixMax (Gmail + Chrome only at time of writing). This can be purchased for as little as $9 a month and gives you the ability to create sequences, track open/response rates to split test emails/subject lines, and ultimately add serious velocity to your prospecting process.

In my opinion, without a tool that gives you both an automated prospecting workflow and insight into what's working so you can fine-tune it, you're going to struggle to be effective with your email outreach.

## Calendar Scheduling Tools

When booking a meeting over email, one of the most frustrating aspects is finding a convenient time. Sure you can suggest a day next week and a time, but if that isn't viable for your prospect you can find yourself playing "email tennis" as you go back-and-forth suggesting alternative times and dates. TIP: if you ever find yourself in this situation, just pick up the goddamn phone!

Calendar scheduling tools are a great way to eradicate this problem and there's loads out there. I personally use the HubSpot version as it comes with our CRM. There are many other popular tools including Calendly, Asana, and YouCanBook.me. Almost all have free versions, and paid-for versions can be as cheap as a few dollars a month.

In a nutshell, your tool of choice gives you a unique link that you can share with your prospects, place on your LinkedIn, add to your email signature and so on. When clicking that link the system will provide a live feed of your availability. It syncs with your calendar and presents any open slots. The prospect can then pick a time and date that suits, and you both get "booked" for the next call.

I find there is a trick to using calendar links. When using it on your cold outreach, offer a calendar link as an alternative, not as the sole option. In my experience, if you sign off an initial email with "you can book a call with me here" (with a link to your calendar) the conversions are typically low. It can feel like you're giving an instruction to a prospect and on a cold email that doesn't always go down so well. What I find works best is still offering a time and a date but in addition, a line like this:

"If that time/date doesn't work, feel free to pick an alternative, here's a link to my calendar".

If you're going to use calendar links heavily, you must ensure your calendar is up to date, which is easier said than done. For instance, you need to block out travel, preparation time for other meetings, lunch breaks and so on.

**Micro Gifting**

Platforms like Reachdesk and Huggg.me let you send your prospects "micro gifts" as part of your outreach (think coffee vouchers, cinema tickets, muffin baskets and so on).

The idea is that you can ask your prospect if they'd like to have a call over a coffee with a link to a free coffee voucher, or tie it somehow to your product.

While I haven't dabbled in it myself, I have been the recipient of a few micro gifts such as a free movie and brownies. Who can say no to free brownies?

**Refract**

At this stage, I think it's only fair we get a chance to plug Refract!

*Refract for Sales Reps*

From an individual rep's perspective, Refract will help you be more successful in sales, earn more commission and get the promotion. The platform gives you the ability to reflect on your own sales calls and demos – helping you understand how you can improve your sales conversations and outcomes.

Who doesn't want to close more deals?

Refract will analyse your call/ demo recordings for you and share key insight which will help you figure out what's happening on your calls. For example, you can see your talk vs listening %, understand the topics you spend most of your time talking about, and see the number of questions you ask. In addition, you can compare your call data with colleagues and understand what top performers are doing differently in their sales calls. Alerts from successful sales calls which ended in booked meetings or deals, are automatically triggered to Slack channels or emails. Learn what's working in real time!

As an added bonus, Refract also takes care of your meeting notes. With a system like this, you can focus on the call itself rather than scribbling notes. After each call/demo, Refract provides you with a copy of the recording with all the key moments in conversation highlighted for you. This means you can quickly revisit the parts where your prospect discussed their problems or goals as well as identifying where budgets/ timeframes were mentioned, and what the next steps were.

Refract also acts as a library of best practice. In your shared library you'll find entire recordings and snippets from your team's calls that demonstrate best practice such as call openings, objection handling and so forth. Access to this library means you can teach yourself and become a top performer in no time

## *Refract for Managers*

For managers, Refract works with your CRM and Call/Demo Recordings and unearths the key moments and trends, helping you find the exact moments when revenue is won and lost in your reps' customer conversations and understand the reasons too. This insight helps you deliver powerful feedback and improve your team's sales conversations and outcomes.

Regular coaching will see you completely eradicate common mistakes and missed opportunities as well as capture, profile, share and double down on what works. Refract makes coaching more efficient and effective, with all the hard work traditionally required to review call/demo recordings removed.

Rich, Stu and I have never had any formal sales training. We are however coached every week.

Between the three of us, we have worked in sales for almost 40 years. We've learnt more in the last few years at Refract than anywhere else.

We wouldn't be the sales leaders we are today without the regular coaching we've received, the Refract platform being key to this, along with the investment of time from our CEO, Kevin Beales.

Coaching works. Most managers just don't do it. They say they don't have the time, when often it's a lack of ability and/or commitment.

Refract removes the excuses.

If anyone reading this would like to learn more, head to www.refract.ai and book a demo.

# Chapter Seventeen

# Prospecting Games to Drive Activity

In our chapter on Cold Calling we talked about the importance of mindset. Prospecting, particularly on the phone requires both mental resilience and commitment. It can be a tough slog and may feel highly repetitive. In order to combat this, we've introduced various games while prospecting, to inject a much needed dollop of fun and an element of competitiveness to help fuel our activity. Here's a selection of games we've played as a team while hitting the phones.

## Heads up

### You'll need

- Pen
- Stickers that you can write on/ sticky notes

The "task master" is responsible for thinking up a celebrity/character for each sales rep. These are then written down one-by-one on an individual sticky note and placed on a rep's forehead, without them seeing their own note.

As an example you might choose David Beckham, Mickey Mouse, The Queen, Homer Simpson or Arnold Schwwarzenegger.

Reps now have a "Power Hour" cold calling session and in this time they're rewarded for their success on the phones.

- If they speak to somebody (regardless of the call outcome) they get to ask one question and/or have one guess at whose name is on their head.
- If they book a meeting with an ideal prospect they get to ask three questions and have three guesses.
- If they obtain a referral they get to ask two questions and have two guesses.

The questions a rep asks can only be closed questions with yes/no answers.

If you're looking to speed the game up, you can have the rule that they can keep asking until the answer is "no" and the one, two or three questions obtained can be lifelines. For instance, you book a meeting, then you can keep asking questions until you've had three "no" responses.

Example questions they can ask:

- Am I a celebrity?
- Am I alive?
- Am I female?
- Am I on TV?
- Am I a sports star?

The game ends when the first person correctly guesses whose name is written on their forehead. You can of course keep playing for 2nd and 3rd place etc.

## Play Your Cards Right/ Card Sharks

This is a re-imagined version of the popular British and American TV show Play your Cards Right/ Card Sharks

**You'll need**

- A pack of playing cards
- Not essential but it helps – a good *Bruce Forsyth impression. ("didn't he do well"?!)

Get your reps enrolled on a cold calling "Power Hour" and when they have success you invite them to 'COME-ON DOWN!!!'

A rep will then play "Play Your Cards Right/ Card Sharks" with you playing the host, 'Bruce'.

Here's what the host needs to do

- Give the deck a good shuffle
- Lay five cards out in a row, face down.
- From the pile of unused cards, turn the card on top over

The first card turned over from the deck is the sales reps' starting card.

The sales rep can choose to stick with this card or swap it. If they swap it, bury this card and take the next card from the top.

Let's imagine they have the Seven of Diamonds.

The host now asks them if they think the first card in the line of five is higher or lower than a seven. If the rep says "higher" and the first card is the Nine of Clubs which is higher than a seven, they get to continue playing.

In this scenario the host would now ask the sales rep if they think the second card in the line of five is higher or lower than the Nine of Clubs. If they say higher and the second card turns out to be the Queen of Spades for example, the rep is right and they get to continue.

The aim of the game is to get five right answers in a row. If at any point the rep is wrong, it's game over and they return to the phones. You can extend the game by simply saying the sales rep who wins the most games wins.

In my opinion, the key to this game is the Host. As the Host, you really need to get into the role and spirit (think 90s game show host – lots of energy and enthusiasm), and that will bleed out into the reps as they watch and cheer as well as "smile as they're dialling"..

Here's' the rules we'd play:

- If a rep speaks to somebody (regardless of the call outcome) they get 0.5 lives
- If they book a meeting with an ICP they get 1 life
- If they obtain a referral they get to 0.5 lives

To play the game, you need one life. Feel free to change the reward system to speed up/slow down the game.

## Grand National

**You'll need**

- Print and cut out an image of a horse for each rep
- Print and cut out of an image of each sales rep's face, the funnier the better (see what you can find on their social media accounts) & stick it on the horse.
- A line drawn across a whiteboard (or similar) to symbolise the race track with markers i.e. 5 points, 10 points etc.

You then place all horses at the starting point and begin a cold calling "Power Hour". The winner is whoever gets to the end of the line first, or in the lead when the session finishes.

Horses move along the race track based on a reps success on the phones.

Here's how we reward success at Refract

- If they speak to somebody (regardless of the call outcome) they move forward by one
- If they book a meeting with an ICP they move forward by three
- If they obtain a referral they move forward by two

Feel free to adjust the number of points awarded to speed up or slow down the game.

## Snakes and Ladders

### You'll need

- A Snakes and Ladders board
- Print and cut out of an image of each sales rep's face for counters: the funnier the better

(see what you can find on their social media accounts)

**Examples below**

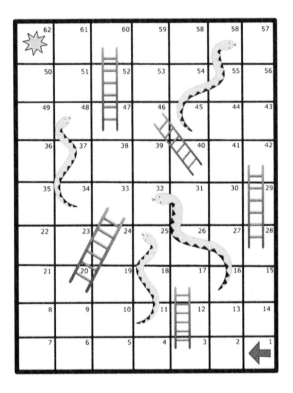

You place all counters at the starting point and begin a cold calling "Power Hour". The winner is whoever gets to the end first, or is in the lead when the session finishes.

Counters move along the board based on a rep's success on the phone. If you land on a snake's head, you go back to the bottom of the snake's tail. If you land on the bottom of a ladder, you move to the top. (I'm sure we've all played this before right!)

Here's how we reward success at Refract

- If they speak to somebody (regardless of the call outcome) they get one roll of the dice.
- If they book a meeting with an ICP they get three rolls of the dice.
- If they obtain a referral they get two rolls of the dice.

Feel free to adjust the number of rolls if you need to speed up or slow down the game.

# Summary

Thanks for reading our book. As we said at the start, our aim here was to give something back and elevate the profession, while helping fellow salespeople like you become more confident and successful.

We genuinely believe we've shared every tip, trick, play and piece of advice we can on prospecting. We've crafted, borrowed or fine-tuned all of these over the years. And we still use them every single day and preach them to our sales team. We know they will serve you well too.

Here's our parting advice...

Take everything in this book and apply it to your own prospecting efforts, but don't sit back and relax thinking you've got it nailed. Everything can be improved.

Never stop prospecting. No matter how senior you get, no matter how busy you are, you should always find time for generating new conversations, and creating pipeline. There's a saying in sales: "nothing happens until something is sold": and while that's fair, as we said at the start "nothing happens in sales until you generate an opportunity".

Continue to invest in yourself and your development. Find and follow other sales leaders on LinkedIn. Read other books, listen to podcasts, attend other webinars and network. Study your colleagues, listen to their sales calls, and read their outreach emails. Understand what it is they do differently in their conversations which makes them successful. Above anything else, take action and put what you've learned into practice!

Never think you've made it. Never think you're too good to improve. The world's very best in any discipline continue to study, learn, and train every day. There's a horrible stigma in sales that implies some people are too good for coaching/training and this is often found in low-performing, but "experienced" sales reps.

If your current employer isn't providing the environment or culture that helps you to improve as a professional, then you need to consider whether it's the right place for you.

If you're in a position where the shoe is on the other foot, and sales reps are prospecting you, remember what it's like to be them. When you pick up the phone and hear a sales rep asking you for "thirty five seconds" or similar, why not just give it to them? We're not saying you have to respond to every email and take every meeting. We're just asking you to treat them with respect.

Be proud of this great profession and see it as your responsibility to encourage and highlight the many benefits of a career in sales to others.

From all three of us, we want to thank you for purchasing and reading this book. If you feel it's helped you improve, then we'd love to know about it. We encourage you to connect with us on LinkedIn and, if you'd be open to it, spread the word by helping us to help others, by leaving a review on Amazon and telling your friends.

Best of luck in your sales careers. We trust prospecting will no longer be a problem...

Mark, Rich, Stu

# About the Authors

## Mark Ackers

Mark Ackers is Head of New Business at Refract

Starting off his career in Marketing he quickly realised sales was where he wanted to be and with the encouragement of his boss he quickly made the change and has never looked back.

Mark's predominantly worked for small 'start up' SaaS companies. His passion is generating new business and all of the elements it comprises, from prospecting to closing.

Mark, originally from Essex, now lives in Newcastle upon Tyne with his wife Michelle and son William. Outside of sales he's a fan of Manchester United, Red Wine, The US Office TV show and Cooking - as seen on Come Dine With Me...no, he didn't win! (2nd!)

## Richard Smith

Richard Smith is Co-Founder and Head of Sales at Refract.

Like many in sales, he fell into the profession after leaving University with an underwhelming Computer Science degree. He has performed all sales roles from lead generation to revenue contributor, and now leads a growing team. He is passionate about coaching and developing others, particularly those just starting their career.

Rich lives in Yorkshire with his wife Ashley after growing up in Newcastle-upon-Tyne and doing a lengthy stint in London. Outside of sales, he's an anguished Newcastle United fan, enjoys craft beer, and his claim to fame is that his parents once won a speedboat on retro UK TV game-show Bullseye.

# Stuart Taylor

Stuart Taylor is Head of Sales Development at Refract

Stu has been in sales for well over a decade. In his early years he was keen to earn as much money as possible which naturally found him end up in sales.

Having sold everything from finance to £100k sports cars, he's certainly learned the hard way how to be successful. Early in his career he won an all expenses paid trip to Las Vegas for being the top performing sales person in the country for Barclays Bank.

His career in sales hasn't always been smooth sailing though. He was once accused of kidnapping Premier League footballer Cesc Fàbregas whilst working for his beloved Sunderland AFC.

When he's not selling or coaching his team, Stu can be found in God's country (Sunderland) with his wife Leanne and new born baby Sophia.

Printed in Great Britain
by Amazon

65375822R00180